The Perfection of Our Faithful Wills

The Perfection of Our Faithful Wills

Paul's Apocalyptic Vision of Entire Sanctification

by Nicholas Rudolph Quient

WIPF & STOCK · Eugene, Oregon

THE PERFECTION OF OUR FAITHFUL WILLS
Paul's Apocalyptic Vision of Entire Sanctification

Copyright © 2019 Nicholas Rudolph Quient. All rights reserved. Except for brief quotations in critical publications or reviews, no part of this book may be reproduced in any manner without prior written permission from the publisher. Write: Permissions, Wipf and Stock Publishers, 199 W. 8th Ave., Suite 3, Eugene, OR 97401.

Wipf & Stock
An Imprint of Wipf and Stock Publishers
199 W. 8th Ave., Suite 3
Eugene, OR 97401

www.wipfandstock.com

PAPERBACK ISBN: 978-1-5326-5623-1
HARDCOVER ISBN: 978-1-5326-5624-8
EBOOK ISBN: 978-1-5326-5625-5

Manufactured in the U.S.A.   DECEMBER 4, 2019

To Kitty

Contents

Acknowledgments | ix
Introduction | xiii

1. What is Christian Perfection? | 1
2. The Image of the Unseen God | 8
3. The Perfection of Our Faithful Wills | 46
4. Sex & Sanctification in Pauline Perspective | 70
5. In the End, God | 87
6. Answering Questions & Objections to Christian Perfection | 99

   Conclusion | 111

   Bibliography | 115
   Author Index | 121
   Scripture index | 125

Acknowledgments

The genesis of this book harkens back to a time of deep personal discontent. I had turned in my final paper on Colossians & Philemon to Dr. Marianne Meye Thompson at Fuller Theological Seminary in the winter of 2018, and was lounging in a coffee shop—as someone my age (twenty-nine at the time) and personality type (INFP) is prone to do—and like almost all of my friends I had no clue about my future as a recent seminary grad. So, I submitted a book proposal and three months later, I was graciously offered a chance to write it. Never make plans in the dark—sometimes God grants them!

But the birthing process of this project cannot be commented on without first thanking those who have shaped me deeply over the course of the past ten or so years. My mentors at Fuller were deeply influential upon my thinking, and chief among them was Dr. Love L. Sechrest, now Vice President for academic affairs and Associate Professor of New Testament at Columbia Theological Seminary in Georgia. Her passion, kindness, and remarkable scholarship has empowered me to return to Paul time and time again, and I owe her a world of thanks for her encouragement and her Christian witness on my life. Hopefully, this work reflects in small part the best of what you imparted to your students. Thanks for being you, Doc.

The other professor who has impacted my life and vocation is Dr. Ronald Pierce at Biola University. It was not until I took his theology of gender course that I began to take seriously the impact of Scripture upon the lives

ACKNOWLEDGMENTS

of people in and outside the church, and thus changed my mind and heart concerning my former restrictive view of women in ministry—hopefully this book matches Dr. Pierce's own passion for empowering women and men to serve together in whatever calling the Holy Spirit has gifted them. Thanks, Doc.

Similarly, the conversations I had with Dr. Tommy Givens, Banning Cantarini, and Chad Dusatko at Fuller Theological Seminary during our directed study on Paul, Judaism, and eschatology were hugely informative on my scholarship, and my friendship with all three continues to breathe fresh air into my life. For my friends David Sidebotham, Trevor Stewart, Johnathan Pritchett, Flow, Chris Loewen, Kyle Christian, Graham Ware, CJ, Nick Stewart, Thomas Horrocks—I'm blessed to call you my friends and fellow theology nerds—and don't worry, I know many of you disagree with me about this issue. I don't hold that against you. A few special notes of thanks go out to Brian Roden and Austin Burgard, who carefully read an early draft of this manuscript and with typical wisdom and wit noted my many mistakes, and to Pastor Austin Long for his insights on patristic sources. Any remaining mistakes are, of course, my own, as much as I would like to think otherwise.

I owe a debt of gratitude to St. Barnabas Church in Pasadena, California. You were my spiritual home for over three years while I was at Fuller. Whether sitting and taking communion, or laughing with John Goldingay, Kathleen Scott, Miss Silvia, Miss Violet, Deacon Jamie, Miss Louise, and Rev. Mark Bradshaw over birthday cake, or cooking breakfast once a month, I am grateful for your witness and kindness and friendship over my seminary time. I came to spiritual fruition because of your witness. May this work be a small reminder of my affection for all of you.

Similarly, I am indebted to the First Baptist Church of Redlands, California—the church where I am blessed to now serve as an associate pastor. The Rev. Dr. Shawn Zambrows has been an empowering force in my life as I serve and teach in this wonderful church, and I cannot imagine a better place to begin my vocational ministry! There are simply too many to name at this wonderful church have welcomed me and comforted me and empowered Allison and myself through the joys and trials of life and ministry and I am forever grateful. I'll see all of you on Sunday.

My sincere thanks to Berva Smith of the First Baptist Church of Redlands for her incisive and wise edits, counsel, and encouragement during the early drafts of this work—without her gifts, this book would be in shambles! Her good humor, encouragement, and wisdom were immeasurably helpful during this time and still remain close to my heart.

It cannot be unstated that I would not be here with the encouragement of my parents Brian and Kim Ahern. Your love of Scripture is a gift given to me, and while I may have fought it a bit in my teenage years, your continual witness to the goodness of God finally won my heart. Your perfect loving kindness exemplifies the kind of parent I hope to be. Also, thanks to my sister Noell for our laughs and snarky times.

For my wife Allison, mere words cannot describe what you mean to me. So I shall not try. You will have to ask me about them when I get home.

Introduction

"Why are you writing a book about *that*?" I recall I was sitting in a coffee shop with a friend, who had expressed interest in the stack of books on my table. When I mentioned I was beginning to research and write a volume on "Christian perfection," he responded with confusion and a bit of his customary candor.

"Does that mean you think you are perfect?"[1]

Immediately, the conversation turned onto various elements of our past sins (with an eye no doubt cast toward our future sins), and the force of my research was set aside in favor of more relevant conversation. But that exchange stuck with me: "So do you think you are perfect?" In essence, it was believed that I had an elitist spirit and was looking down upon him from on high. In much of evangelical discourse, we are firmly set in certain ideas and established patterns of thought, with little genuine exploration of sanctification and other related issues from unexpected corners of Christendom.[2] Sanctification, broadly defined, is the process by which a person is made holy before God. There are many facets to how this facet of doctrine works but suffice to say we will be focused on final sanctification, which is a journey toward entire sanctification. But we will touch on that later.

---

1. My initial answer was "no"—for the record. It still is.
2. Daniel L. Burnett, *Shadow of Aldersgate*, esp. 116.

INTRODUCTION

In addition to this, numerous questions compound when one considers the scope and intent of sanctification, and how the Holy Spirit can achieve such a result before death. A very personal element at the heart of this question is the quest for rectification and reconciliation in a world steeped in violence, sexual misconduct, pride, and isolation: how does the Christian live her life in concert with the calling of God in Christ by the Holy Spirit? How does one's journey culminate in this life? In being called to pastoral ministry and the academy, I have sensed a tension many have felt, and part of my goal is to argue that what one does in the academy should be easily translated to the body of the local church. I write this as a licensed minister, a man who has placed himself in obedience to Scripture and the history of the church universal, and I am deeply aware of the sins of the church. But, this book is for both the church and is an attempt to call the church into a life of holy love—a holy and undeniable love for both God and for our neighbors.

It was only when I took a Greek class on Philippians and Philemon under Dr. Love Sechrest at Fuller Theological Seminary that I considered the implications of this debate, and concluded that Christian perfectionism is a perfectly biblical notion that deserves a place in the wider debate in New Testament theology, especially in Pauline studies. The doctrine does not undermine any specific Christian doctrine and requires a robust view of, say, the doctrine of sin and anthropology. This doctrine, at its most base level, cannot exist without a doctrine of the Trinity and is therefore grounded entirely within the best of the Christian tradition. By the grace of God, I hope to persuade you of this. If you are not persuaded, I hope that you will be challenged to further pursue holiness in the sight of God in the presence of Christ by the power of the Spirit. Wesleyan theologian William J. Abraham astutely notes,

> We are so far removed from the originating doctrine of Christian perfection that retrieving it for the purposes of exposition is a challenge. John Wesley's vision of Christian perfection is an exercise in ascetic theology, a vision of realized eschatology, and a psychology of spiritual development. The ascetic element in the doctrine insists that a robust form of perfection is the goal of Christian existence under grace.[3]

Abraham is not the first one to make this well-founded claim, although he is perhaps the most outspoken. W. Stanley Johnson also claims that

---

3. Abraham, "Christian Perfection," 587.

INTRODUCTION

> The growing conviction that love for God is central to Wesley's idea of perfection stands in the uneasy company of a nagging suspicion that current theological literature and much preaching from the holiness pulpit has missed the Wesleyan and Biblical emphasis upon love for God.[4]

The debate of Christian perfection is, thus, no longer confined to Reformed or Baptist or Wesleyan circles. Many Wesleyan's have written on this topic, and H. Ray Dunning is perhaps the most concise when he states, "It is generally recognized by insightful analysts of the Holiness tradition that this movement is in the midst of a serious identity crisis."[5] Rather, the languishing of the doctrine has occurred especially within a theological tradition that was its original source. I hope the present work matches the challenge stated by those such as Abraham, Johnson, and Dunning.

The concept of "perfection" today is often considered to be a source of much consternation for the average Christian. Some assume this ancient doctrine of Christian perfection to be, at best, deeply offensive to their present theological sensibilities and, at worst, a blight on the theological map and thus a threat to Christian faith and proper formation. For instance, Reformed theologian R. C. Sproul states quite emphatically, "the peril of perfectionism is that it seriously distorts the human mind."[6] Similarly, Reformed theologian Wayne Grudem writes, "there does not seem to be any convincing verse in Scripture that teach that it is possible for anyone to be completely free of sin in this life."[7] In other words, ought does not imply can.[8] As one can see, "perfection" is not a common or desirable soteriological option for many Evangelical brothers and sisters—I know I found the doctrine deeply disconcerting once I heard about it, as previously mentioned. However, I have since changed my mind, and I hope to change and challenge these misconceptions in a spirited and respectful way. This work will cut through the caricatures of our present theological discourse by offering a theological vision that does justice to the criticisms while seeking to be faithful to the words of Scripture, offering a Pauline vision of total sanctification and its possibility in this life. Ultimately, this work will

---

4. Johnson, "Christian Perfection," 50.
5. Dunning, "Christian Perfection," 151.
6. Sproul, "Heresy of Perfectionism."
7. Grudem, *Systematic Theology*, 751.
8. One can see echoes of the Reformed or Calvinistic objection as being located by the use of this isolated idiom. C.f. Horton, *Christian Faith*, 667.

present a brief defense of the Wesleyan view of entire sanctification and introduce a unique Pauline interpretation. This will be accomplished by first offering up several axiomatic points or themes that provide a framework for reading Paul in this chapter. Chapter 2 will specifically focus on Paul's theology of divine Christology, which will provide an initial axiom for theological fruition; this includes an exposition on the doctrine of Christ as the grounds by which perfectionism can be achieved. Then it will be argued that Paul's theological anthropology requires a transformation of the whole person, set forth by the sovereignty of the Holy Spirit. Thus, the final question in chapter 2 will surround Paul's view of the human "will" or "mind," and how this will affect sanctification in the following chapters. Together, these axioms provide a lens by which we may then view ethics and sanctification.

Chapter 3 is the largest and perhaps most controversial chapter, where I will argue that Paul believed that "perfection" was possible in this life. I will argue primarily from the Pauline Epistles, with additional theological and historical arguments to bolster my case: specifically from John Wesley and the work of others like William J. Abraham and Kenneth J. Collins.[9] An essential component of this chapter is the belief that Paul's theology can largely be described as "apocalyptic," and this will require some specific definition of this modern scholarly debate. Chapter 4 is perhaps less overtly controversial; in there I focus on the ethical nature of Paul's theology in relation to his view of "perfectionism:" specific topics include marriage, sex, creation, and purity as they all relate together: Paul's ethics are, in my perspective, fundamentally somatic. Chapter 5 is centered on Pauline eschatology in relation to "perfection," which includes the reconciliation of the cosmos, the renewal of creation, the annihilation of death and human wickedness, and Paul's vision of a liberated cosmos. This, in essence, is where the entire work is teleologically oriented: the utter annihilation of sin and death, and the righteous display of God's goodness in creation, the hope of eternal life. How is God at work in our broken world? Chapter 6 is dedicated to answering various theological objections to "perfectionism," whether from Reformed or Wesleyan scholars, particularly in the realm of biblical and systematic theology, as these two disciplines are often at odds

---

9. I will respond to exegetical arguments against Christian perfectionism in chapter 3 exclusively (for example, the arguments made by commentators on the Greek text), although my responses to the more popular arguments will be saved for chapter 6.

with one another.[10] Chapter 7 is a summarizing conclusion, tying up any loose ends, and offering a vision for women and men in ministry and for lay people about how they might disciple one another in their gifts, to the glory of God, to the perfection of their faithful wills in Christ. I will also include some thoughts about how men and women might preach this doctrine. All theology is for the growth of God's people, and if doctrine does not abound in doxology, what good is it? This is a doctrine that should be preached to the glory of God, for the glory of God's people.

> *And can it be that I should gain*
> *An interest in the Savior's blood*
> *Died He for me, who caused His pain*
> *For me, who Him to death pursued?*
> *Amazing love! How can it be*
> *That Thou, my God, shouldst die for me?*
> *Amazing love! How can it be*
> *That Thou, my God, shouldst die for me?*[11]

In essence, rather than providing a multi-volume work, I am writing a short Pauline theology with the doctrine of entire sanctification as my guiding light. It is my hope that you will, like me, be convinced. Or, if not convinced, then at the very least, be inspired to reconsider what is possible in the Spirit as we seek sanctification "in the fear of God."

—NRQ
Eastertide 2019
Redlands, California

---

10. That is to say, exegesis and theology are two hands that a Christian ought to use to construct a vision for the Christian life.

11. https://hymnary.org/text/and_can_it_be_that_i_should_gain.

1

What is Christian Perfection?
Questions & Foundations

> "There is scarce any expression in Holy Writ which has given more offence than this. The word perfect is what many cannot bear. The very sound of it is an abomination to them. And whosoever preaches perfection (as the phrase is)—that is, asserts that it is attainable in this life–runs great hazard of being accounted by them worse than a heathen man or a publican."
>
> —JOHN WESLEY, *SERMON ON PERFECTION* 40

In his seminal sermon on Philippians 3:12—a major "perfectionist" text that will be discussed in chapter 3—Anglican preacher John Wesley seems to express some reticence concerning this doctrine, but mirroring the mentality of Saint Paul in Galatians 1–2 he writes: "We may not, therefore, [because these words are written in Holy Scripture] lay these expressions aside, seeing they are the words of God, and not of man."[1] In other words, Wesley was convicted that although this doctrine was perhaps offensive to some, it was also necessary for the church. As a result, he continued to preach it, even against all odds. He begins by addressing the negative, or

1. *Sermon on Perfection* 40.3.

the aspect concerning "in which sense Christians are not perfect." Grider describes a multitude of terms used to describe the preferred "entire sanctification." They include "perfect love," "the second blessing," "the second work of grace," "Christian holiness," "the second rest," "heart purity," and "the fullness of the blessing."[2] Now, with these nuances in mind, we will first turn to Wesley's positive case about what Christian perfection actually *is* after we have laid aside some of the misunderstandings.[3]

Wesley asserts that Christians "are not perfect in knowledge . . . [or] free from ignorance."[4] He is quick to insist that humanity is utterly incapacitated by sin, unable to "search [God] out to perfection" or, in other words, to the fullest sense possible. Human beings, by nature, are mortal and frail, subjected to sin and death. Hence, "no one, then, is so perfect in this life, as to be free from ignorance,"[5] or rather, mistakes. All people make mistakes and lack the principle "facts" of what entails the truths about the universe. So John Wesley is not addressing the "mistakes" or "ignorance" of Christians; rather, he argues that many can continue in these ways, but this is not itself necessarily sinful: " the best of men are liable to mistake, and do mistake day by day."[6] This may include even "error" or "bodily infirmities,"[7] and Wesley exhibits a special tenderness especially towards those with mental illness, as these human beings are obviously excluded given their limited moral capacity for willing sinfulness. Wesley states, "From these [bodily infirmities] none can hope to be perfectly freed till the spirit returns to God that gave it [Ecclesiastes 12:7]."[8] In relation to the future eschatological reality of God's kingdom, Wesley asserts, "nor can we expect . . . to be wholly free from temptation." That is to say, That is to say . . . "perfection does not denote the absence of temptation and the like in 'this life.'"[9] Abraham wisely concludes, "The overarching ascetic vision was set within the Christian narrative of creation, freedom, fall, and redemption that informed his Trinitarian theology as a whole. He also knitted his doctrine of perfection

---

2. Grider, *Wesleyan-Holiness*, 367–78.

3. For a condensed and helpful summary that follows this same paradigm, see Collins, *Scripture Way*, 171–82.

4. Sermon 40, I.1.

5. Sermon 40, I.4.

6. Sermon 40, I.5.

7. Sermon 40, I.7.

8. Sermon 40, I.7.

9. Sermon 40, I.8.

seamlessly into a robust vision of human happiness. So there is no need to call into question the orthodoxy or the humanity of Wesley's views."[10] John Wesley, as it were, operated hermeneutically with "resolute Biblicism."[11] However, Wesley sees all of these various negative facets as being irrelevant to Christian theology. For him, much of the misunderstanding is due to the mistaken assumptions of his readers and listeners. "Indeed, [Christian perfection] is only another term for holiness."[12] Holiness is not primarily about the future: perfect holiness is about human participation in the life of Christ right *now*. The journey of holiness begins now. Eschewing the nature of being holy in the present world as regards sex, love, marriage, creation care, and economics cannot survive sincere scrutiny—we are to be holy as an imperatival necessity now: be holy now as God is holy always. As such, holiness begins at conversion.

Building positively upon his previous clarifications, Wesley asserts that there is a progressive journey or "stages in Christian life,"[13] offering a helpful distinction between babies and adults:[14] "for [the latter] only are properly Christians."[15] This is not exclusively a theme noticed by John Wesley or propagated by Paul. As initial prolegomena or theological exposition, it must be noted that the language of "perfection" is not limited to Paul; rather such language is a definitive and pervasive New Testament theme. That is to say, the doctrine[16] cannot be extracted on the basis of mere prooftexting, as if citing a singular verse apart from broader theological considerations is somehow theological meritorious. As such, it is important to note "Wesleyans do not come to their biblical understanding of sanctification by a system of logical deduction from certain proof texts or propositions." But their understanding emerges "out of their attempt to see Scripture holistically."[17] The classic text on perfectionism is Matt 5:43: "Therefore, you shall be perfect (τέλειοι) as your heavenly father is perfect (τέλειός)." Jesus in the Gospel of John speaks of "perfecting" or "completing" [τελειώσω] the work"

---

10. Abraham, "Christian Perfection," 588.
11. Abraham, "Christian Perfection," 589.
12. *Sermon* 40, I.9.
13. *Sermon* 40, II.1.
14. *Sermon* 40, II.1.
15. *Sermon* 40, II.2.
16. One might also assert that no doctrine should fall into this type of methodological vanity.
17. Dieter, "Wesleyan Perspective," 30.

of the Father (4:34; 5:36; 17:4)[18] and the people of the Father (17:23). The author of Hebrews also speaks in a similar manner of the people of God becoming "perfect through sufferings" (2:10), and of Christ's own perfection (7:19) of his people (10:14). The author of 1 John sees the perfection of "love" being or occurring "in us" (2:5; 4:12, 17, 18), which extends far beyond any notion of goal: the moral and spiritual dimensions according to 1 John are communal and formative. So Paul is operating with a similar ideological mindset when he writes about "perfect," illustrating continuity with other writers of Scripture. This brief distillation of the wider data of the New Testament is meant to illustrate that the concept is not confined to Paul, but Paul is the principal source of "perfectionism," especially as it relates to the outworking of Christian theology and the Christian life.

For some within the Reformed side of the Christian family, perfection is closely related to "the eschatological prospect: the goal of perfection,"[19] and so the concept of perfection does not seem, at least initially, to present any sort of issue for Reformed theology—especially if one has a high view of the doctrine of the Holy Spirit, properly conceptualizes Christian perfection, and is willing to offer detailed and innovative approaches to old questions.[20] As such, Christian perfection is certainly a Wesleyan distinctive but, as we shall see, I do not believe it is antithetical to Reformed theology. However, one must resist the impulse to "eschatologicalize" sanctification in punting such practical divinity into the nebulous and unyielding "end," especially if one professes the sovereignty of the immanent and dynamic triune God. That is, it is a mistake to make the pursuit and goal of holiness an entirely eschatological event.

Wesley notes the beginning of what he calls "outward sin,"[21] building his argument principally from Romans 6, especially v. 11: "dead unto sin, and alive unto God."[22] This speaks of "not [sinning] willfully . . . or habitually."[23] If one wanted to press for a more modern idiomatic phrase, one could say a Christian does not sin with a high hand, or to intentionally act upon their desire to participate in sin. The concept of "interchange" in Christ is perhaps a necessary outworking of Wesley's theology, where the

18. Thompson, *John*, 107–8.
19. Berkouwer, *Studies in Dogmatic*, 109.
20. See the work of Crisp, *Saving Calvinism* and *Deviant Calvinism*.
21. *Sermon 40* II.4.
22. *Sermon 40* II.4
23. *Sermon 40* II.6.

person forgoes the means of sin and the pursuit of godless desire. However, it does not follow necessarily that the presence of sin in the life of the believer immediately renders the doctrine inert: the instantaneous transformation of our mortal bodies into vehicles of purity is not done overnight—at least as far I can see. There may be instances where the Spirit works with surprising effectiveness (as the Spirit is wont to do) but this does not appear to be the regular method of perfection.[24] The late Methodist theologian Thomas Oden rightly notes, "the faithful are not perfect in knowledge nor free from weakness, finitude, or temptation, but the Christian life aims toward unblemished love of God and neighbor that is not intrinsically unrealized . . . it is not a static notion but rather dynamic, a *teleiôsis* and not a *perfectus*."[25] For Wesley and much of the Wesleyan tradition, however nuanced and variegated, this distinctive doctrine is defined "as an instantaneous cleansing from Adamic sin, and am empowerment, which Christian believers may receive, by faith, through the Baptism of the Holy Spirit."[26] This is the definition offered by J. Kenneth Grider in his monograph *Entire Sanctification: The Distinctive Doctrine of Wesleyanism*, written in 1980. Of course, it can be debated about the timing and effect of this "instantaneous cleansing,"[27] as much of modern Methodist and Wesleyan theology has shown.[28] It can take a lifetime of holiness and seeking the goodness of God by the power of the Holy Spirit. Sin is great, but the triune God is greater than any Sin. As Wesley himself said:

> The grace of God was surely sufficient for them. And it is sufficient for us at this day. With the temptation which fell on them, there was a way to escape; as there is to every soul of man in every temptation. So that whosoever is tempted to any sin, need not yield; for no man is tempted above that he is able to bear. [^{1} Cor ^{10}:^{13}].[29]

---

24. As such, we should be open to such miraculous events, but I don't see how one can expect such events to occur with any regularity—to expect such a thing would turn the Holy Spirit into a wish-dispensing puppet.

25. Oden, *Christ and Salvation*, 237–66, 240.

26. Grider, *Entire Sanctification*.

27. The question of baptism is also relevant, but perhaps less so than other factors. Baptism is in inauguration of the human person into the sphere of the Spirit and the community of faith, where participation in Christ's life and death and resurrection results in the journey.

28. Often, the chief caricature of Christian perfection is on the assumed instantaneousness of it; we will tackle this objection in chapter 6.

29. *Sermon* 40, II.14.

To give an example: a husband and a wife, united in holy marriage before God and the church, are far different from the people they will be in ten years, or twenty years, or fifty years. I am not the same man I was when I married my wife, Allison—we can both praise God for that, I am sure. I was often cold, quiet, and lacking the ability to communicate. While one cannot say that I have been sanctified of such things, one can say that the journey is real. The journey of entire sanctification, by the power of the Holy Spirit, is the presence of actual change and growing holiness in the life of the Christian, with the end result that the desire for sin will be replaced entirely by holy love. Pain and trauma and grief will—in time—be transformed into an undying holy love that seeks rectification instead of retribution. It does not mean all Christian men and women will obtain perfection in this life, but it does mean that we are to hope for and participate in our perfection through Christ as his body, and, by the power of the Holy Spirit, sanctification can be completed in this life.

The principal conclusion is that "Methodism preached a vision of perfection as a real possibility for all believers here and now; it offered entire sanctification for the masses rather than postpone it till death or limit it to the chosen few in the monastery."[30] If perfection is possible for all people, then spiritual dominance and theological hierarchicalism cannot thrive. Holiness is for *all* people: for people who struggle with pornography, sexual immorality, violence, anger, vengeance, hatred and for people with seminary degrees and people without seminary degrees, and so forth. Holiness is egalitarian—it affects everyone and yet draws all people toward the holy love of God, where mercy is found (Rom 3:25). As Kenneth J. Collins helpfully states, "Entire sanctification, then, is love replacing sin, love conquering every vile passion and temper."[31] In the helpful survey *Key United Methodist Beliefs*, William J. Abraham and David F. Watson remind us that this doctrine is not centered on the human person's ability to save himself or herself. Rather, "Our wills align with God's will . . . perfection only makes sense if we remember that it is God's doing, not our doing."[32] Self-perfection is an oxymoron, untenable as a Christian doctrine. It is an unlivable lifestyle that shirks all notions of community and fellowship and discipleship. Rather, the human person is utterly reliant on the work of the eternal Son, who is the image of the unseen God (Col 1:15). All Christian

---

30. Abraham, "Christian Perfection," 597.
31. Collins, *Scripture Way*, 176–77.
32. Abraham and Watson, *Key United*, 78.

doctrine is dependent upon the person of Christ, who he was and who he is, and it is in light of this eternal Son that we should see who we really are.

2

The Image of the Unseen God
Apocalyptic Christology & Anthropology

2.1: Apocalyptic Now: Definitions, Contours, & Relevance

A theologian once told me, "Apocalyptic is an adjective, not a noun."[1] As is customary, attempting to define words used in different ways by theologians and biblical scholars is a bit like trying to corral an angry cat. But we persist. Apocalyptic may describe a social movement (the Qumran community), a type of literary genre (the book of Daniel, 4 Ezra, 2 Baruch), or more specifically, a worldview. For instance, apocalyptic eschatology is concerned with the final vindication of God in God's final triumph over the cosmic powers of sin and death. Described and defined this way, "apocalyptic" is an epistemology or worldview, not a literary genre or a social movement. John J. Collins defines "apocalypse" as

> A genre of revelatory literature with a narrative framework, in which a revelation is mediated by an otherworldly being to a human recipient, disclosing a transcendent reality which is both temporal, insofar as it envisages eschatological salvation, and spatial insofar as it involves another supernatural world.[2]

---

1. Dr. Michael F. Bird, in a personal conversation in January 2018.
2. Collins, *Apocalypse, Prophecy*, 4–5.

When considering the genre of a specific text, Collins' definition is suitable and helpful. He rightly emphasizes the nature of the genre of a given Second Temple text and, in essence, helps move the modern scholarly use of the term "apocalyptic" in a more precise direction. Simply put, much of the modern use of the "apocalyptic" adjective has shifted toward being concerned with Barthian categories and less concerned with Second Temple Jewish sources. The literary content of Romans or 1 Corinthians has not been categorized as apocalyptic in terms of genre, but in terms of worldview—Collins has rightly called this thematic collapse into question, especially in any way that divorces modern apocalyptic theology from first-century Jewish thought. For instance, the late J. Christiaan Beker of Princeton Theological Seminary rather famously characterized Paul's "apocalyptic gospel" as "vindication, universalism, dualism, and imminence."[3] In doing so, one can see a shift in terminology away from the literary genre of "apocalyptic," and Beker's move toward a Pauline epistemology and worldview was essential for this distinction. For Beker, and subsequent apocalyptic interpreters of Paul like J. Louis Martyn, Douglas A. Campbell, and Beverley Gaventa, the nature of a literary genre discourse was set aside in favor of certain textual elements and specific theological themes, although there is debate concerning the "narrative" character and shape of Paul's theology.[4] Beker, and subsequent interpreters focused on the hyper-fundamentalism of their time, perhaps best exemplified by Hal Lindsey's *The Late Great Planet Earth*. For my purposes, I will be using the adjective "apocalyptic" to describe the quality of Paul's epistemology: *how* he thinks about God, Christ, and the end of evil in the world now, as opposed to the future, undefined eschatological reality that lies at the center of much of pop-eschatology. In essence, "apocalyptic" in this work is surmised in the realm of Christology and the work of Christ in and for the life of the body—the invasion of Christ into our lives is a call to holiness and liberation from the powers. New creation is the impulse and integrity of the Christian hope for entire sanctification, bringing humanity into willing conformity by the Spirit.[5]

---

3. Beker, *Apocalyptic Gospel*, 30–53.

4. It must be noted that it depends on what Epistles one accepts as Pauline. The diverse, disjunctive and ad hoc nature of the Pauline corpus is intensified if one accepts for example the Pastoral Epistles as Pauline in comparison to Romans or 1 Corinthians or Colossians. For much of the established apocalyptic school, Romans and Galatians have very clearly been privileged and undeservedly so.

5. Wright, *Rethinking Heaven*.

2.2: Apocalyptic Christology: The Self-Impoverishment of the Son of God

When attempting to construct a mere sketch of Paul's Christology, one is forced to omit or condense various aspects and images from the portrait. Whether one is talking about preexistence apart from incarnation, or the humanness of Jesus as opposed to his equality with the Father, one is always wary of the variegated elements of Paul's christological outlook and how they play off one another without eclipsing the whole. The purpose of all scholarship on Pauline Christology is to allow each element its due respect and expression: for in doing so, each image and concept will more fully illuminate the other.

Pre-existence & Poverty. In much of the modern world, poverty is a problem in the process of being undermined and attacked. In the ancient world, poverty was an ugly existence inherited by the vast majority of the population,[6] and the early Jesus movement was not immune to this inhuman reality. This awareness comes across most clearly in the Epistles of Paul, particularly in his discourse about financial giving in 2 Corinthians 8. Paul begins by expressing thanksgiving for "the wealth of their generosity" (τὸ πλοῦτος τῆς ἁπλότητος αὐτῶν) in 8:2, which he hopes Titus will "fully complete" (ἐπιτελέσῃ: 8:6b). This entire pericope (vv.1–11) is centered on Paul attempting to persuade the Corinthians, who are in poverty, to keep giving whatever they can without forceful coercion or cultural manipulation. The crucial example of this selfless giving (emptying) is demonstrated by the gift of Christ in 2 Corinthians 8:9: "For I want you to know the gift of our Lord Jesus Christ, who because he was wealthy became impoverished [ἐπτώχευσεν] for your sake, so that you might be enriched by his poverty [πτωχείᾳ]."

It has been classically argued that this act of becoming "impoverished" (aorist verb: ἐπτώχευσεν) refers to the incarnation of Jesus, in the act of emptying himself of his divine right as the eternal Son. In seeking to enrich those who are sacrificing what little wealth they have, Paul characterizes the eternal Son as being wealthy before his self-imposed impoverishment. However, not all accept this reading. For example, James Dunn believes that "the most obvious way to take 2 Cor. 8:9 is as a vivid allusion to the tremendous personal cost of Jesus' ministry and particularly the willing

---

6. Longenecker, *Remember the Poor*.

sacrifice of his death."⁷ Hence, for Dunn, Paul is about the historical life of Jesus as opposed to Jesus' forsaking his divine rights in a preexistent state of equality with God the Father. Similarly, Jerome Murphy-O'Connor states, "such a meaning [an incarnational understanding of 2 Cor 8:9], however, has no basis either in Paul's theological perspective or in the immediate context."⁸ That is to say, the incarnation of the preexistent Christ is separated from the impoverishment of the Corinthian church. For those concerned with both Christian perfection and the preexistence of Christ, this will not do. For Murphy-O'Connor, the text under question refers to "the radical impoverishment" of Christ as human.⁹ Christ, in essence, is the ideal human being for this view, and thus the incarnation is placed outside the scope of interpretive options. Several factors make the non-incarnational reading unlikely. First, the patristic consensus on this appears to be decidedly in favor of viewing this act of impoverishment as the incarnation. For instance, in his *Exegetical Homilies*, Basil the Great (330–379) focuses on the specific phrase in Psalm 33:7 during his sixteenth homily: "This poor man cried, and the Lord heard him." As has been seen, poverty in the ancient world was a way of life for the majority of the populace, and sometimes the element of poverty was seen positively insofar as it was adopted "intentionally." Basil pursues this line of reasoning christologically, stating that the poor man is a "disciple of Christ." His citation of 2 Corinthians 8:9 is preceded by a commentary on Christ "being rich by nature." Basil's emphasis on the deliberate "choosing" of poverty is seen as a blessing: "he [the poor man] who has considered the command of Christ better than the treasures of the world." Meekness and self-impoverishment are thus preferable to extreme wealth. Basil's Christology is thus guided not necessarily by participation, but imitation: the person who actively chooses poverty is imitating Christ, who likewise chose poverty, an act of extreme humility. Poverty is only valuable or noble if it is freely chosen. Of course, this begs the question on the nature of ancient poverty, especially since most people are not born into extreme wealth. Basil is not ignorant of this. However, the exemplary Christ answers this question for Basil, bringing liberation to those who participate in him.

---

7. Dunn, *Theology of Apostle*, 292. It must be said that this "non-incarnational" view may not represent Dunn's personal view, only his view on what Paul said and believed.

8. Murphy-O'Connor, *Theology*, 83.

9. Murphy-O'Connor, *Theology*, 83.

A second reason to reject the non-incarnational reading is that we have no record of Jesus ever being wealthy in the synoptic tradition; thus, the claim that this "impoverishment" must refer to his human impoverishment simply lacks sufficient evidence from the Synoptic Gospels. A third reason outside of the various patristic readings and the lack of evidence for Jesus' wealth from the Gospels is this: the concessive participle ὤν ("who being") reflects a state of existence [that is defined by wealth or riches] *before* his act of personal abasement.[10] Paul nowhere speaks of Jesus as being wealthy before his death: the riches of Christ are displayed only upon his death and resurrection. If the action of "becoming impoverished" (ἐπτώχευσεν) means the apocalyptic reciprocal enrichment of the believers in Corinth, then the only plausible meaning is that Jesus' incarnation was revealed in the glorious invasion of what it meant to be human: utter destitution, utter desolation, from the heights of glory to the depths of enslavement and deprivation, from being the eternal Son to being a slave within the universal realm of poverty. That is to say, Jesus Christ entered into the human condition at the lowest level of society: enslavement and impoverishment. The Son did not come on the wings of chariots, nor did he prize himself as being worthy of never setting foot on soil. Rather, the impoverishment talked about by Paul reflects his belief that Jesus was like humankind in every way, and God did not hide himself from the agony of what it means to be human. The prospect of eschatological "riches" for those who are impoverished is also exemplified in the Testament of Judah 25.4:

> Those who died in sorrow shall be raised in joy, and those who died in poverty for the Lord's sake shall be made rich; those who died on account of the Lord shall be awakened to life.

The notion of recapitulation or vindication on the part of those who were faithful to God is not to be missed, especially when compared with Paul's language here. The One who was wealthy beyond comprehension in God-status is enfleshed among us as one of us. As John Wesley states so eloquently: "in becoming man, in all his life; in his death: rich . . . in the favour and image of God."[11] So despite their well-constructed arguments, Dunn and Murphy-O'Connor appear to be within the minority report of New Testament scholarship on this verse. Most modern New Testament

---

10. Martin, *2 Corinthians*, 263.
11. Wesley, *Explanatory Notes*, 462.

commentators[12] have pushed back against this thesis, and Margaret Thrall is the best representative. She states that the "traditional interpretation [i.e., the preexistence son becoming poor through the incarnation] of the verse is preferable to the other possibilities suggested,"[13] and Dunn's "non-incarnational" option is indeed excluded by her critique. Thrall concludes:

> [Christ's] self-impoverishment in the whole event of incarnation was for the spiritual enrichment of believers. We have the same principle of interchange as in $^{5:21}$. The riches are not further defined and are probably to be understood in a comprehensive sense as all the blessings of eschatological salvation.[14]

N. T. Wright concurs with Thrall, calling the theme of this text "Messiah-shaped generosity."[15] John Calvin summarizes the matter quite succinctly: "Christ was rich because he was God . . . thus he sanctified poverty in His own person, so that believers should no longer shrink from it."[16] In summation, the incarnational reading of 2 Corinthians 8:9 appears to be the preferable option amongst modern exegetes, although there are of course fierce detractors. This presents us with some significant material to work through later in terms of anthropology and how Paul views the nature of the human person in reference to sin and death and materiality. What makes 2 Corinthians 8:9 so powerful is the similarly thematic parallel with a similar text, Philippians 2:5–11, which reads as follows

> [5]*Have this mindset among yourselves, which was also in Christ Jesus,* [6]*who being in the form*[17] *of God did not consider equality with*

---

12. Belleville, *2 Corinthians*, 215–17; Collins, *Second Corinthians*, 171–72; Guthrie, *2 Corinthians*, 406; Harris, *Second Epistle*, 578–79; Martin, *2 Corinthians*, 263–64; Seifrid, *Second Letter*, 330.
13. Thrall, *Critical and Exegetical*, 534.
14. Thrall, *II Corinthians*, 534.
15. Wright, *Paul and Faithfulness*, 1105.
16. Calvin, *Second Epistle*, 110–11.
17. As John Wesley states, this word refers to "the incommunicable nature of God from eternity," as he was afterward in the form of man, real God, as real man (*Explanatory Notes*, 508). In addition to this, some have proposed an Adam Christology at play here. Dunn, *Christology*. Much of Dunn's case relies on questionable parallels, especially given the assumption of a master story concerning Adam. While such parallels are present in Rom 5:12–21, 7:7–25, and 1 Cor 15, it is highly unlikely that he has "Adam" in mind in Phil 2:5–11. A distinct lack of "Adamic" material in Philippians requires us to impute such an understanding here when Adam is nowhere mentioned and remains elusive. The search of Paul's master narrative continues.

> God something to be preserved [for himself].[18] [7]But he deprived[19] himself instead by taking the form of a slave, being born in the likeness of humanity, [8]and being found in appearance as a human being, he abased himself, becoming obedient to the point of death—even a death on a cross. [9]For this reason, God supremely exalted him and granted to him the name above every name [10]so that by the name of Jesus every knee among the heavenlies and the earth and the subterranean realm might bow [11]and every tongue may confess that Jesus Christ is Lord for the glory of God the Father.

For the purpose of this volume, I am more focused on the nature of impoverishment in vv. 6–8. As with 2 Corinthians 8:9 we see an immediate connection to the concept of "abandonment" or "forsaking" of something. In the case of 2 Corinthians 8:9 it is on the Son becoming impoverished for humanity. In the case of Philippians 2:6–7, it is of a similar track. He "deprived himself" (αυτὸν ἐκένωσεν) of his former state/status with God the Father, releasing himself from the privilege of being immune from humankind. Rather than remain in a state of glory and equality, the Son became unequal, "actively taking" (λαβών) the form of a slave—the lowest realm of human suffering and inequality.[20] The use of the middle verb γενόμενος ("being born": v.7)[21] does not work as a statement merely of human birth apart from preexistence, as the previous actions illustrate agency in "depriving himself" of something before he is even born: to suggest otherwise appears incoherent.[22] Rather, the Son deprived himself of his previous glory and equality and accepted the task of being a slave and, as a consequence, was born through Mary.[23] To rest on this for a moment, the ancient perspective on slaves is almost wholly negative. Pliny the Elder asserts that it is because of the inferiority of slaves that "there are no famous works of art, nor statues, made by anyone who was a slave" (*Natural History* 35–36). To be a slave was to be a body, a living tool.

---

18. The precise meaning of this noun (ἁρπαγμὸν) is disputed. The noun can either refer to an act of robbery, or a thing grasped. As I have translated the term, I have tried to make sense of both meanings. See the discussion in Fee, *Paul's Letter*, 204–7.

19. Literally, "emptied."

20. The contrast between "equality with God" and "the form of a slave" is meant as stark opposites: no greater chasm exists between God and a human slave, that is, until the Son became incarnate.

21. See the similar language in Gal 4:4 and the Son "being born."

22. That is, how did the unborn empty himself before being born?

23. As Matthew W. Bates has persuasively argued: see *Birth of Trinity*, 158–59.

This enslavement to the powers culminates in the utter humiliating murder of the Son (v.8), but the end result is not an eternal reminder of God's abandonment. It is rather the final display of God's glory in raising his vindicated Son from the grave (1 Tim 3:16). The text speaks profoundly in terms of Christo-centricity about the nature of being human (i.e., enslavement) and the willingness of the Son to embrace a debased identity that not even his enemies would expect.[24] Christ sacrificed all of the privileges and blessings of heaven to participate fully in human existence. As such, Christian perfection becomes a far more compelling doctrine when it is applied to Christology: the perfect one comes, nestles among us, suffers the depths of depravity Rome could inflict, and rises to glory vindicated by God—a perfect life so that we might participate in this life of suffering and glory. The immeasurable faith of Jesus Christ is a central part to this, as it requires Jesus to know exactly what it means to be human, and to that end, what it means to be faithful despite suffering and pain. As the perfect One, Jesus did not privilege his own life even unto an unholy death, so that we might participate in his perfect life by the power of the Spirit. Therefore, Christ's faithful allegiance[25] to God is an important element of Christology and one that we will now explore.

Faithfulness & the Human One. If my reading of both 2 Corinthians 8:9 and Philippians 2:5–11 is true, then the additional element of Jesus' faithfulness plays a large role in understanding his actions as the human One. Several Pauline texts remain central to Jesus' faithfulness in his human life. Romans 5:19 directly utilizes the language of "obedience" (ὑπακοῆς) concerning Jesus' human life in contrast with the power of sin and death. This sort of language is used early in Romans and also in Galatians. Both Romans 3:22 and Galatians 3:22 uses a specific grammatical phrase that has been highly debated in recent Pauline studies. The Greek phrase is πίστεως Ἰησοῦ Χριστοῦ and can be translated in two general ways:

- "Faith in Christ" (called the objective genitive; our faith in Christ)
- "Faith/fulness of Christ" (called the subjective genitive; Christ's own faith)

---

24. See the masterful exploration of this text in Gorman, *Inhabiting Cruciform God*, chapter 1.

25. In terms of "faith," I will sometimes use the language of "allegiance" as a synonym, based on the excellent work done by Bates, *Salvation by Allegiance*.

THE PERFECTION OF OUR FAITHFUL WILLS

Grammatically, both interpretive options are certainly plausible and arguments have been marshaled in support of either perspective.[26] Without seeking to break any new linguistic ground, I believe the subjective genitive reading of both Romans 3:22 and Galatians 3:22 is the most plausible understanding of these two texts, although I do not believe that Christ faith excludes synergism or human participation.[27] Hence, the "righteousness of God" is displayed and demonstrated by means of the allegiant faithfulness of the Son: the righteousness of God tells us more about the character of God in terms of covenantal faithfulness and apocalyptic rectification. Or to put it another way, the means of displaying God's apocalyptic righteousness was exacted in the person of Jesus Christ (Rom 1:17: possibly echoing Habakkuk 2:4 LXX). In Galatians 2:16, the faithful person is "rectified" (δικαιοῦται) not through "works of law" but "through the faithfulness of Jesus Christ" (διὰ πίστεως Ἰησοῦ Χριστοῦ: Gal 2:16a). Christ, as the one who lived a perfect life in allegiance to God, is the North Star to our theological journey. His faith gives us the grounding for our own faith in him. His faith becomes our standard of faithfulness: through his faithfulness we see through the lens clearly.

The body of Christ is integral to Paul's Christology, especially as it relates to identification with the corruptibility of the human condition and to our participation in bodily resurrection. Jesus' faithfulness as the human One exemplifies the perfection of Jesus as the one who dwelt as the Deity in bodily form (Col 2:9).[28] His resurrection affirms the dignity of both male and female, as both are raised without the obliteration of their bodies. Hence, the element of incarnational perfection includes the self-impoverishment of Jesus, his eternal preexistence and equality with the Father and the Holy Spirit, and his subsequent life of perfect faithfulness. Included in incarnational faithfulness is not blind adherence to a proposition. It is not a christological triumphalism that eschews the reality of pain or grief or trauma; rather, the impoverishment of the eternal Son contextualized grief and declares that he hasn't hidden himself from such things, and that such things have their end in him. Specifically, we see Jesus' own desire for deliverance from death (Luke 22:42), and perhaps his recognition of

---

26. Bird and Sprinkle, eds. *Faith of Jesus*.

27. Without endorsing everything therein, see the arguments by Campbell, *Deliverance of God* passim.

28. "For in him all the fullness of deity dwells bodily" (ὅτι ἐν αὐτῷ κατοικεῖ πᾶν τὸ πλήρωμα τῆς θεότητος σωματικῶς). Fee, *Pauline Christology*, 505.

doubt (which reminds us that doubt is not opposed to faithfulness) can be included in the journey toward greater truth and clarity. "I have faith—help my lack of faith!" (Mark 9:24). How did God express solidarity and identification with us? He became one of us, like the least of us, so that we might see who God truly is and what God truly desires (1 Tim 2:4-6).

Resurrection & Enthronement. While there are debates concerning preexistence in Philippians 2:5–11 and 2 Corinthians 8:9, some of the most significant interpretive issues lie at the very beginning of Paul's most contested and beloved Epistle, Romans. The first few verses of Romans can be translated as follows (1:1–4):

> ¹Paul, a slave of Christ Jesus, a called apostle, set apart for the Gospel of God, ²who was promised beforehand through his prophets in the Holy Scriptures ³concerning his Son, the one who was born (γενομένου) from the seed of David according to the flesh (σάρκα), ⁴who was appointed Son-of-God-in-power (ἐν δυνάμει) according to the Spirit of Holiness (ἁγιωσύνης) by (ἐξ) his resurrection from the dead: Jesus Christ our Lord.

Where the Greek text follows the English translation, therein lies the most disputed elements of Romans 1:3–4. Many think Paul is quoting a creed or a "protocreed,"[29] but this debate does not appear particularly relevant to our immediate concerns. The problem arises most clearly when stated by Robert Jewett: "the adoptionist Christology of primitive Palestinian Christianity implied in Acts 2:36 and 13:33 surfaces in this formulation."[30] How does the language of "come into being" and "appointed Son of God" coalesce with the language of preexistence and equality found in Philippians 2:5–11, as well as the rest of the Pauline corpus?

What is compelling is Paul's use of the articular participle τοῦ γενομένου functions substantivally: "the one being born/coming into being,"[31] which clearly refers to a human birth, but the substantival participle also might refer to a new *form* of existence. The referent is clear: "seed of David," along with other keywords, denotes the material sphere of political influence, in accordance with kingship and messiahship. As is common with birth, "flesh" (σάρκα) is an appropriate moniker to describe the newborn human

---

29. Bates, "Christology," 107–27, 108.

30. Jewett, *Romans*, 104.

31. The fact that Paul uses the middle/passive does not diminish the agency of the Son, as we've seen in Phil 2:6-8. Porter notes that this verb is a "frequent verb of existence." Stanley E. Porter, *Letter to Romans*, 45.

person, and "flesh" (=humanity) is described in contrast (but not in opposition to) "spirit" (πνεῦμα) in v. 4. As Matthew Bates has pointed out, "rather [according to Paul's use of the verb under question], the emphasis is normally on change in status or mode of existence."[32] In short, Jesus was always God's Son, whether in the preexistent realm or the material realm (ἐκ σπέρματος Δαυὶδ κατὰ σάρκα = sphere of flesh/Messiah). The Son entered into a new mode of being/incarnate (τοῦ γενομένου) and was granted "kingship" upon his resurrection from the dead.[33] The vindication of the Son's human life, which is not to be divorced from his pre-existent state, is at the heart of this text: thus, inherent within Paul's use of the participle is the assumption of preexistence and the Son's activity in becoming incarnate, a point made with equal force in Galatians 4:4. The mere fact that the Son entered into σάρκα enforces the thesis that the perfection of the Son is assumed before, during, and after his incarnation, and Mary's role in his birth and life cannot be dismissed.[34] As Michael Bird notes, "the parallelism between v.3 and v.4 is not antithetical, but marks a narratival progression as God's Son shifts from exercising his messianic mission in human weakness to his newly acquired divine prerogatives of power in his post-resurrection state."[35] A life lived in perfect weakness and powerlessness is vindicated and demonstrated in final exaltation by the resurrection, where Jesus' lordship reigns over the violent power of Caesar and continues to reign until the end.

Thus, the adoptionist argument concerning Romans 1:3-4 should be viewed as an unstable hypothesis.[36] Jesus' rulership here is set forth as a thematic link toward Christ's rulership over death and sin in Romans 5:12-21, where we "reign in life because of Jesus Christ" (Rom 5:17, 21). The Holy Spirit is also at work in the power of the resurrection.[37] In contrast

---

32. Bates, "Christology," 115.
33. See the excellent work by Jipp, "Ancient, Modern," 241-59.
34. Bates, "Christology," 119-20.
35. Bird, *Jesus Eternal Son*, 16-17.
36. Similarly, in 2 Tim 2:8, we have the same sort of phrase: "from the seed of David" (ἐκ σπέρματος Δαυίδ), which stresses the messianic aspect of Paul's Gospel and his Christology.
37. The Greek πνεῦμα ἁγιωσύνης could be a reference to Jesus' spirit of holiness in terms of his earthly life, or to the Holy Spirit. Given the Proto-Trinitarianism of Paul's theology, especially in Rom 8:1-11, the Holy Spirit is perhaps the implied πνεῦμα ἁγιωσύνης who had a hand in resurrection. This same Holy Spirit will be active in our resurrection as well (1 Cor 15:35).

to the empires of the world, then and now, Jesus remains King and Lord and it is only through his faithfulness that we have any hope in participating in his resurrection. These two verses, when taken together, do not present Christians with the option of adoptionist Christology: rather, we see the messianic Son as the eternal Son, where both his humanity and his preexistence are held together in two clear verses, and they fold within one another in a concise and compact manner. The humanity of Jesus is not collapsed into his divinity, nor is the humanity of the Son contradictory to his divinity. Rather, the Son was always in essence perfect—without moral flaw—and did not cease to be perfect in his incarnate state. The notion of recapitulation

Additional notions of kingship and Christ's reign are present in Philippians 3:20–21,[38] particularly as it relates to "citizenship" (πολίτευμα)[39] or a populated enclosed region:[40] "For our citizenship is in the heavens, and from there we eagerly anticipate a Savior, the Lord Jesus Christ, who will transform our humiliated body into being conformed to his body of glory according to the working of his power, and to subject all things to himself." Christ's reign in the "heavenlies" (ἐν οὐρανοῖς) is characterized in terms of "deliverance" (σωτῆρα): the one who will deliver those who are his people or citizens. In some sense, the reign of Christ in the heavenly places speaks to multiple spatial metaphors: he reigns on high, and that is where our citizenship resides (Col 3:1–4), and additionally we see Paul's politicized set of terms "savior/deliverer" (σωτῆρα) and "Lord" (κύριον). Christ's reign is heavenly, but Christ is not going to bring his "citizens" up to himself;[41] rather his "citizens" are waiting for him to return, as the preposition ἐξ denotes and we "eagerly anticipate" (ἀπεκδεχόμεθα) his apocalyptic return. Christ's kingship is wrapped up entirely in his own bodily presence, specifically because our citizenship is wrapped up in him. Our participation in Christ's kingship and vocational calling: our body (corporately) will be like his (individually): this is no kingly reincarnation or transference of a "soul" to the body. Rather, our "humiliated bodies" (v. 21) are parallel to Christ's own incarnational "humiliation" (Phil 2:8), and thus we see an

---

38. The implications of this text will be explored further in subsequent chapters.

39. Louw-Nida offers the following gloss: 1.88 πόλις, εως *f*: a population center, in contrast with a rural area or countryside and without specific reference to size—"city, town." In classical Greek, the word group is most often associated with city-states.

40. See the use of the word in 2 Macc, especially 2 Macc 12:7.

41. The spatial element of Christ returning "from" the heavenly realm is not to be equated with elements of the "rapture."

equivalency between humiliation and glory—instead of a King ruling with violent prejudice and unrestrained desires and maliciousness,[42] we see a King who would enter into the human sphere of existence, suffer as we suffered—impoverished and broken—and then he resurrected unto glory for our sanctification and rectification. We see a perfect King. The resurrection of the body is God's final verdict in favor of a sinful humanity; the resurrection of the body is God's display of glory in making beautiful things out of us. No Caesar or Hitler would ever become like the least of his community, no tyrant would forsake himself to an accursed cross. Yet, as Scripture tells us, Jesus dared to do just that. "Any humiliation an empire might place on the bodies of the faithful will be transformed and redeemed by the power of the resurrected Christ."[43] Jesus' power to "subject" (ὑποτάξαι)[44] all things, which echoes the principalities and powers motif, is similar to God's own power in 1 Corinthians 15:20–28 and perhaps Romans 8:20, which reads: "For creation was subjected (ὑπετάγη) to futility, not voluntarily but because of the One who subjected it (τὸν ὑποτάξαντα) in hope."[45] Naturally, the question arises: is "the One who subjects" a reference to God,[46] Christ, or the Godhead?[47] We have seen previously and clearly that Christ has the power to "subject" all things in Philippians 3:20–21, and God the Father has this same power in 1 Corinthians 15:25–28. Stanley Porter helpfully summarizes the issue in Romans 8:20: "most commentators understand it [that is, the one who subjects] as God, even to the point of calling it a 'divine passive.'"[48] While helpful, this explanation does not necessarily give one a specific answer if we affirm that the Son is divine or even called God

---

42. Mark 10:40.

43. Fowl, *Philippians*, 175.

44. The language of "subject" or "subordination" is used in a variety of contexts in the New Testament and in the wider Jewish world. We will encounter this word in our discussion later on gender and sanctification, but it must be said that a context of kingship and rulership is not equivalent to the marriage relationship in terms of style, grammar, and application.

45. The use of τὸν ὑποτάξαντα is similar to the articular substantive participle in Rom 1:3–4 (τοῦ γενομένου: "the one coming into being"), reflecting agency on the part of Jesus Christ.

46. For instance, Jewett, *Romans*, 513–14 affirms this point as does Longenecker, *Epistle to Romans*, 722–23.

47. That is, God as revealed as Father, Son, and Holy Spirit.

48. Porter, *Romans*, 168.

in Romans.⁴⁹ Nor does it suggest that divine authority is limited to either Father or Son. However, in light of the Trinitarian⁵⁰ language in Romans 8:9–11 where the Spirit of God (8:9b) and the Spirit of Christ (8:9c) are active, and in the climactic apocalyptic vision of resurrection, the Father who raised the Son from the dead will also bring those in the Son back to life through his Spirit (8:11). The reciprocal interaction between Father, Son, and Spirit throughout these three verses suggests a mutual symmetry⁵¹ between the persons of the Trinity in accomplishing the telos of rectification and resurrection. Thus, the Trinitarian nature of rectification and life in the Spirit in 8:9–11 should press us toward viewing "the One who subjected [creation]" (τὸν ὑποτάξαντα) as a reference to the Godhead rather than an exclusive and rather oblique reference simply and exclusively to the Father.⁵² This suggests that the Holy Spirit is also included in the activity of redemption. This sort of "kingship" and "subjection" language is present throughout Second Temple literature (2 Macc 8:9, 22) and the Greek First Testament (Ps 17:48 LXX). Rather than being a game of singular power or sole rulership, the mutual interworking⁵³ of the Godhead is on full display here.⁵⁴ Jesus' "body of glory" in Philippians 3:21 is reminiscent of the perfection he had before creation and his resurrection: the glory of the Son was not exchanged for a new and different glory, but rather glory is given within

---

49. Rom 9:5, which more likely refers to Jesus as θεός ("God"). See the reasonable discussion in Jewett, *Romans*, 566–69 in favor of Jesus as θεός. As we have seen above, there is no specific reason to exclude Jesus' equality with the Father unless one believes Paul is incapable of doing such a thing.

50. Scholars often use the modifier "proto" in relation to Trinitarian language, but I do not find it to be a useful modifier. Paul's Trinitarianism is remarkably coherent for how little we allegedley see of it.

51. To borrow the language from Hill, *Paul and Trinity*, 61–64; see especially p.120 for this helpful phrase to describe 1 Cor 15:20–28.

52. This is the power of theological interpretation and dogmatic theology in combination with biblical exegesis: when considered and implemented together, the mutual strengths become both apparent and necessary.

53. It seems that the pronoun αὐτῷ is reflexive, referring to Christ's own work in subjecting all things to himself instead of God for at least two reasons: first, the lack of a direct referent to God (that is, the Father) makes the simple pronoun reading difficult—it would be an incredibly oblique reference to God. Second, in rejecting subordinationist Christology, I see no issue in any person of the Trinity exercising power and authority in communion with the Godhead.

54. This sort of perspective is also evident in Wesley Hill's work, *Paul and the Trinity*. I will be reliant upon his work below.

the realm and reality of resurrection-power.⁵⁵ The perfection of the Son is a return to perfect glory, a prince returning home in honor and power.

A similar text already briefly mentioned concerning enthronement Christology is found in 1 Corinthians 15:20-28:

> ²⁰but now Christ has been raised from the dead, the first fruits of those who have died, ²¹for since Death came about through a person, the resurrection of the dead came about through a person. ²²Just as in Adam all die, likewise in Christ all will be made alive. ²³But each one in their own order: Christ the first fruit, then those who are Christ's in his return. ²⁴Then the final End: when he hands over the Kingdom to God, even the Father, after he has annihilated all rulership and all sovereignty and power. ²⁵For he will continue to reign until he has placed all of the adversaries beneath his feet. ²⁶The final enemy to be utterly annihilated is Death. ²⁷For God has subjected all things beneath his feet, but when it says, "all things have been subjected," it is clear that the Father has not been subjected to him in all things. ²⁸And when all things have been subjected to him, then the Son will subject himself to the one who subjected all things to him, so that God might be all in all.

There is a sense of mutuality present even here, as the Father places "all things" beneath the Son and the Son himself submits himself to the Father in the narrative of apocalyptic rectification. As with the expression and exaction of sovereignty by both Father and Son elsewhere, we see the same sort of reciprocity between the Son acting as sovereign King and the Father acting as sovereign King—the apocalyptic kingdom is shared explicitly by both Father and Son in Ephesians 5:5-6, so the Son offering back the kingdom is not the equivalent of purging himself of his sovereignty or equality.⁵⁶ We are not free to argue in an exclusive manner that "God is the one who

---

55. The patristic readings of Rom 8:20 do not center on the question of "who" precisely subjected creation. Their focus is on the nature of the word "futility." Many of them simply used the language of "Creator," which can apply both to Father or Son, depending on the context. My thanks to Pastor Austin Long of Gapway Baptist Church, North Carolina for pointing this out to me.

56. It might also be noted that when Paul speaks of the Son not subordinating the Father in v. 27b, he appears to be inferring that the Son could have placed the Father beneath his feet, but the Son does not. The Father is "excluded" from enforced subjection. Nowhere does the Father explicitly subject the Son: rather, the Son submits mutually to the Father in offering the kingdom to him. Submission, in Trinitarian contexts, does not infer an authority relationship, as equals are free to yield to one another.

defeats [Death]."⁵⁷ Rather, the power of the Son in "continuing to reign" is an assertion of mutual activity between Father and Son in resurrection, rulership, and the annihilation of that final enemy, the enemy to end all enemies, death. The removal of the final "sting" of death is a Trinitarian effort. Christ's rulership in 1 Corinthians 15:24–28 is an "expanded description of the surrender of the kingdom already mentioned . . . this means that the identity of Christ in v.28, although ordered asymmetrically with God's identity, is inseparable from that of God as his Father."⁵⁸ The Son cannot exist without the Father and the Spirit, and likewise the Spirit and the Father. Thus, we do not have here a unilateral activity of power *over* another, but an act of divine yielding *to* one to another for the purpose of being "all in all." The culmination of all of God's actions in redemptive history centers on how God responds to evil, and how this affects our journey into Christlikeness. Freedom from sin entails the removal of walls and barriers (Eph 2:11–22) and God is in the present working to undue such realities. Christ's kingdom in his post-resurrection stage is that of rulership over all the adversarial sovereignties (both material and immaterial) for the purpose of destroying them and restoring the cosmos to its rightful place under the Godhead.⁵⁹ Christ's willful⁶⁰ submission in taking the role of redemption does not apply ontologically, but temporally, to the course of cosmological rectification.⁶¹ As his incarnation was freely assumed, so too is his future yielding of the kingdom. The questions of God's final response to evil, sin, and death (annihilation, eschatological torment, or universalism) as a result of this sort of christological apocalypticism are to be reserved for a coming chapter. The Father and the Son are distinct from one another, yet united in mutual purpose in achieving the liberation of the cosmos, and the reign of the Son does not conflict with the reign of the Father. Verse 25 speaks of the Son subjecting all things and v. 27 speaks of the Father also subjecting

---

57. Garland, *1 Corinthians*, 713.

58. Hill, *Paul and Trinity*, 128–29, 129.

59. Christ's own subjection is also a future aspect in v. 27, which may suggest that the Son is not subject presently in his present resurrection state. My thanks to Dr. Cynthia Long Westfall of McMaster Divinity College for pointing this out to me in private conversation at the Christians for Biblical Equality Conference in Orlando, 2017.

60. Submission, even in other contexts, is used in the middle sense (that is, reflexive) to suggest the self-agency of one party submitting to another (Eph 5:21–24).

61. Another major dispute concerning this pericope is on the extent and modification and application of Ps 8:7 and 110 in these verses. The most compelling reading is, again, offered by Hill, *Paul and Trinity*, 123–27.

all things under Christ, and we must be careful not press temporal willful subordination on the part of the Son (see the exegesis of Phil 2:6–8 above) into an ontological category that annihilates the unity of the Godhead, especially for the purpose of a social or ecclesiological agenda.[62] God is One and remains One in the purpose of rectification, and the kingdom of God is Trinitarian in all its glory and goodness.

In terms of exaltation, we see similar language in Ephesians 1:20–23 and 5:5, and also in Colossians 1:13–20: when taken together we see the same sort of mutuality and unity in the Godhead, especially as this subject relates to the kingdom and Christ's enthronement. We will now briefly address Ephesians 1:20–23 and 5:5:

> [20]*Which he worked through Christ having raised him from death, and seated him by his right hand among the heavenly places* [21]*high above all rule and sovereignty, power and lordship, and every name being named—not only in this age but even in the coming age.* [22]*And he has subjected (ὑπέταξεν) all things beneath his feet, and he gave him as head (κεφαλὴν) over all things for the sake of*[63] *the church,* [23]*which is his body, the fullness of him, the one fulfilling all in all.*
>
> [5:5] *For this you surely know: that everyone who is sexually immoral or unclean or engaged in avarice—which is idolatry—does not possess an inheritance (κληρονομίαν) in the Kingdom of Christ and God* (ἐν τῇ βασιλείᾳ τοῦ Χριστοῦ καὶ θεοῦ)

In terms of enthronement in Ephesians, Paul's vision of Christ is asserted as being "over" or "above" (ὑπὲρ) all foreign sovereignties, and this has political connotations especially as it relates to the divine name (Phil 2:9–11 above). The name of Jesus is greater than the name assumed or designated to various emperors—even Caesar himself. Rather than the body being discarded

---

62. This criticism applies both to so-called complementarians and egalitarians who would seek to wield the Trinity as a weapon to promote or exclude women from ministry. Such a debate must be done on other texts, and I write this as a convinced egalitarian who does not affirm the eternal subordination of the Son, and I am not alone in seeing no connection between the Trinity and ecclesiology. See Bird and Harrower, *Trinity*.

63. The lack of a designating preposition in relation to Christ as κεφαλὴν to the church suggests that τῇ ἐκκλησίᾳ is a dative of benefit: that is, Christ is κεφαλὴν over all things "for the sake of the church, his body." One could also argue that Christ, *with* the church, is head over all things. Christ's headship is relegated to being enthroned and exalted over the various powers and sovereignties, and his relationship to the church takes on a different form, where head/body metaphors suggest an organic or somatic unity not predicated upon authority (Eph 4:14–16; 5:21–33): see Westfall, *Paul and Gender*, 92–95, 100–2.

or denigrated, Christ's headship is the provision and care he shows as the church's benefactor.[64] Christ's rulership over the entire cosmological spectrum extends across the expanse of time itself ("the coming age"), where his Name is asserted as being "above" all other principalities and thrones and kingdoms: rather the kingdom has two co-rulers in Ephesians 5:5 and the apocalyptic element of Paul's christological press us into seeing reciprocity in the Godhead, especially as it relates to Christian teachings on the Trinity. The use of a sole referent or agent does not exclude the other two persons of the Trinity. In Ephesians alone, Πατήρ ("father") is used eleven[65] times, eight times of God the Father, which suggesting a culturally specific concept of associating divine "fatherhood" with "inheritance"[66] and children. Paul's use of πατὴρ ("father") is likely meant to evoke an immediate kinship response to his underprivileged readers, and the fact that the Son is included in this reigning kingdom removes the exclusivity of a unitarian reading of Paul here in Ephesians 5:5. Sovereignty is co-opted for Paul's Christology and in the apocalyptic landscape, and dogmatic or creedal theology is on solid ground in interpreting the New Testament through the lens of later universal Christian creeds, where even the process of sanctification is centered on divine goodness and benevolence.

Colossians 1:13–20 uses similar language as Ephesians, but the emphasis utilized by Paul is that of a different stripe. Key themes of liberation, body, and preexistence and enthronement are woven together in this key text—more specifically, agency is involved deeply with this text in Colossians.[67]

> [13]*Who has emancipated us from the sovereignty of the realm of Darkness and transitioned us into the Kingdom of his beloved Son* [14]*through whom we have emancipation, the forgiveness of Sins.* [15]*He is the image of the unseen God, the firstborn of all creation.* [16]*For through him all things were created in the heavens and upon the land, things that have been seen or things unseen, whether thrones or Lordships or Powers or Sovereignties—all things were created through him and for him.* [17]*And he is before all things and in him all things are bound together.* [18]*And he is the head of the Body, the*

---

64. Christ is explicitly the "creator" or "source" of the sovereignties in Col 1:16.

65. The other three uses of πατὴρ in Ephesians occur in the *Haustafeln* (5:31; 6:2; 6:4) and clearly are not referring to God the Father.

66. The various cognates of Πατὴρ and κληρονομία occur together many times in the LXX. See Gen 28:4, 31:14; Num 27:11; Jer 3:19 (LXX).

67. We see similar language of "creational agency" in 1 Cor 8:6.

> *church: he is the beginning, the firstborn from the dead so that in everything he might become preeminent.* ¹⁹*For all the fullness of God was pleased to dwell in him.* ²⁰*And through him to reconcile all things for himself by making peace through the blood of his cross, through him, whether things upon the land or things among the heavens.*

Paul's apocalyptic theology shines through in full-force here. He speaks specifically of the Son's kingdom (v. 13b) without specific reference to God's kingdom; this conforms to the notion of co-rulership in the apocalyptic reign of God, for God's own act of transference echoes the story of the First Testament.[68] It is in and through Christ that we have emancipation and forgiveness of sins, and no other being is capable of more fully representing the Father to us, than that of the seen Son (v. 15). The Son's own agency in creating the various sovereignties in v. 16 forces us to consider the idea of Christ's agency in creation, which comports well with the notion of his pre-existence, thus stating the obvious. Christ's position before "all things" (καὶ αὐτός ἐστιν πρὸ πάντων) in reference to creation suggests a time before the incarnation where the Son was in the beginning (echoing Gen 1:1 LXX).[69] As the "firstborn from the dead," the Son is quite simply the perfect representation of the rightful King who reconciles creation to himself. Instead of reducing creation and all human beings and sovereignties to dust, the Father operates through the Son and the Spirit to reconcile all things to God's self, without cause for discrimination or prejudice. The "kingdom of his beloved Son" (τὴν βασιλείαν τοῦ υἱοῦ τῆς ἀγάπης αὐτοῦ) is a present reality, not a future concept. The apocalyptic nature of the invasiveness of God-in-Christ is at work, pulling a group of people from their sin and oppressed state, and offering them asylum in a kingdom of justice and mercy, where reconciliation triumphs over enslavement and domination. In the end, "the triumph of Christ over 'all things' for which Paul hopes, in contrast to Caesar's triumph . . . comes by persuasion and requires the free response of faith and praise."[70]

---

68. Exod 6:6.

69. Gen 1:1 LXX: <u>Ἐν ἀρχῇ</u> ἐποίησεν ὁ θεὸς τὸν οὐρανὸν καὶ τὴν γῆν. The underlined words are words also found in Col 1:15-20, suggesting a thematic and linguistic intertext.

70. Jewett, *Romans*, 569.

2.3: The Reign of the Holy Spirit

For Christians, the Holy Spirit is the agent of God's presence (Ps 51:11), the person who pursues and empowers people toward Christ, sometimes before they are even born (Luke 1:15). In the miraculous event of Jesus' birth by the Virgin Mary, the Holy Spirit is a unique and authoritative agent: in his birth, Jesus is holy because of the holiness of the Father and the Holy Spirit (Luke 1:35). To be God is to be perfect in holiness, in righteousness, and in the totality of their being. The love of God is manifested and fully known by the giving of the Holy Spirit (Rom 5:5). As such, the Holy Spirit is the manifested love of the triune God for all of humanity. The implication of the Spirit's work in creation and reconciliation is woven throughout Paul's Epistles, and the agency of the Spirit is not removed from the work of sanctification. For instance, the physicality of God's kingdom is given a secondary status as holy attributes ("righteousness, peace, joy") in Romans 14:17 are found through the work of the Holy Spirit. the Holy Spirit. Additionally, both the Father and the Holy Spirit share the divine hope as we are filled with peace and hope by both.[71] The Holy Spirit, finally, is the one who sanctifies ("or makes holy") the offering from the people of the nations (Rom 15:16).[72] The interactivity of the Holy Spirit in being present with Jesus in the temptation narratives in the Synoptic Gospels demonstrates the distinction and unity of the triune God.[73] To receive this gift of the Holy Spirit (Acts 2:38) is to participate in being conformed to the image of God's Son. To be empowered and filled by the Holy Spirit is to be adopted into God's family out of enslavement and bondage (Rom 8:15). The work of the Holy Spirit testifies to both the goodness of the triune God and the loving desire of the triune God: to reconcile all things to God through Christ and to empower the church to be God's hands in the world. The work of the Father and the Son is dependent upon the agency of the Spirit, whose name we claim when we baptize one another into Christ (Matt 28:19). Without the Holy Spirit, entire sanctification cannot be enacted—indeed, sanctification as a *whole* cannot survive or persist. That is why we freely cooperate with God as his image-bearers and participate in the union of the Spirit as our guiding impulse toward holiness. Participation in the perfect Christ

---

71. The co-operative work of the Father and the Holy Spirit in this ministry of reconciliation assumes their divinity and shared authority.

72. Additional texts that emphasize the Holy Spirit's role in sanctification and baptism and the call to holiness include 1 Cor 6:11.

73. Matt 4:1; Mark 1:12; Luke 4:1.

means that sin cannot be an ever-present reality. Being conformed to the image of the resurrected Christ is the final undoing of sin in our lives, sealing ourselves in the Spirit for the day of complete redemption. As such, we are called to participate in God's perfect calling.

Perfective Christological Trinitarianism: A Summation. In this all too brief survey, we've seen a mosaic of various christological images and themes presented. Several things, however, seem to be quite clear: Paul's affirmation of the pre-existence of the Son is predicated upon his perfection alongside the Father and the Spirit prior to his incarnation. Upon his apocalyptic invasion into the world, the Son remains without sin[74] although under the power of sin and oppression, in an active state of participatory impoverishment in identification with all humanity. More specifically, "along with a full affirmation of the identification of the human Jesus with our humanity, that identification avoids sinfulness as sin does not belong to the essence of human nature."[75] Upon Jesus' vindication by means of the resurrection, the Son is exalted to the Father's right hand, to the same positional equality he shared with the Father before his incarnation. Throughout this entire apocalyptic redemptive narrative, the Son has never forsaken his perfect status, and this christological status has massive implications for our anthropology and all that follows in this volume. Because of the revelation of God-in-Christ-by-the-Spirit we know of the goodness and the perfection that is the ontic reality of God. God is perfect and has always been so, especially as this perfection relates to God's other attributes—especially holiness and goodness. Jesus became what we are so that we might become as he was. All three persons of the Trinity are free from sin, death, and subjection in their relationship, and it is to their shared glory that they freely and mutually exercise their cooperative actions in service of redemption without tiers or further qualifications.[76]

2.4: The Emancipation of Our Bodies: Paul & the Human Person

The debate concerning Pauline anthropology is a shaky and imprecise affair. For many, the debate can largely be settled through various ingenious

---

74. For a discussion on Jesus and sinlessness, see Kärkkäinen, *Christ and Reconciliation*, 168–78.

75. Kärkkäinen, *Christ*, 178.

76. Butner, *The Son*.

and, I might say, novel appeals to Romans 7. However, we ought to take a larger view of human anthropology in Paul before we engage deeply with Romans 7:7–25.[77]

2.4a: Slavery & Sin

Paul's view of the human person centers largely on the Adamic state or sphere of reality. This "Adamic" reality is comprised of multiple factors, but chief among them are sin (Rom 5:12) and death (Rom 6:6). Adopting the "Adamic" reading of Romans 7:7–13 where Adam is the principle "speaker" in Paul's use of "speech-in-character," we see that sin is an enslaving entity of power (Rom 7:13)—sin enacts and gives fermentation to the agency of death. Rectification or "justification" is the antidote to the imperial or cosmic reality of Adamic enslavement, and Paul's vision of sanctification produces a whole host of possibilities. While Paul can assert that Christ has confronted the social order of enslavement by his own impoverishment (Col 3:11; Gal 3:28), such abolition did not universally occur in Paul's lifetime. However, Paul reconfigures the notion of slavery as it relates to the social order and how it relates to Christ. Being a "slave of Christ" or "slave of God" places someone within the sphere or reality of God-in-Christ. Identity in the Spirit is the direct counter to the imperial order. The domination of the human person as it relates to sin and sinful behavior is something Christ explicitly counters (1 Cor 6:12).[78] For those who have baptized into Christ, there is freedom.

2.4b: Subjection

In conjunction with the imperial order of the "sovereignties," Paul's generally negative view of anthropology places the human person squarely in the fight between Christ and the powers. Christ has been "exalted" over the sovereignties (Eph 1:22), but Satan is the head of the various cosmic agents of chaos in the present reality (Eph 2:2; 6:12). Indeed, Satan is the "god" of this age (2 Cor 4:4). Humanity has been placed within this "Adamic" reality that includes the exercise of sovereignty over the bodies of all human

---

77. Most of the objections to Christian perfection center on a specific reading of Romans 7, and as such I have saved the best for the final chapter.

78. See the discussion in Dunn, *Theology of Paul*, 111–27.

beings, including human enslavement of one another. In the beginning, this was not so. God created humanity in God's own image (Gen 1:26–28) and in what happened after humanity became enslaved to sin and death. Reality has been controlled and subordinated by the sovereignty of the devil, in cooperation with those who willfully participate with the work of the devil, revealing the morass of sin that has enveloped all of humanity. This results in the human person being unable to submit to God's law (Rom 8:7), and this affects the totality of creation (Rom 8:20). The selfish and narcissistic self did not enjoin itself to God's plan of rectification (Rom 10:3) and this anthropological actuality is what Paul is centered upon—especially as it relates to what God has done in Christ as it relates to prevenient grace. Specifically, the notion that in the Son was light and this light is manifested by his incarnational presence, which provides enlightenment for "all humanity coming into the cosmos" (John 1:9). While there is some debate about the grammar of this verse, it seems best to take the language as referring to humanity's response to Christ. Christ provided light and was not overpowered by the darkness. Yet this created realm did not "acknowledge" him. Many did not "accept" him. Yet those who did so by means of this "Christ-enlightenment"—these one's exercising faithfulness to Christ— were gifted with authority to be God's children. The grace of God the Father is manifested in the body of Christ, the one who illuminates all people without distinction. The incarnation is the apocalyptic act of God in creation that provides prevenient grace before humanity enters into the cosmos, dispelling darkness and terror and human selfishness.

2.4c: Suffering, Hope, & Embodiment

> [1] *For we know that if the tent which is our earthly house is destroyed, we have a building from God not made with human hands that is eternal and in the heavens.* [2] *For even in this tent we groan,*[79] *yearning to be clothed by our heavenly home.* [3] *If indeed by being clothed, we are not found naked!* [4] *For we are in the tent and we groan, being weighed down, not that we would be stripped bare but to be further clothed, for the purpose of what is mortal might be swallowed up in Life.* [5] *And the one preparing us for this is God, who has given us the Spirit as a down payment.* [6] *Therefore, be confident always! And know that while we are at home in the body, we are absent from the Lord:* [7] *For we live*

---

79. This verb is used by Paul to refer to the creation itself "groaning" for liberation in Rom 8:23, which also includes the "emancipation of our bodies."

> *by faithfulness, not by what we see* ⁸*and we are confident and we are pleased to be away from the body and dwelling with the Lord.* ⁹*Therefore we aspire, whether we are at home or away, to be well-pleasing to him.* ¹⁰*For all of us must appear in the presence of the judgment seat of Christ so that each of us might be repaid for what was practiced through the body, whether good or evil.* (2 Cor 5:1-10)

Paul has already spoken about those who are "being destroyed" (ἀπολλυμένοις: 4:3), and the context of 2 Corinthians 4:3ff is concerned with suffering and humiliation at the hands of the oppressors. The imagery of "jars of clay" (ὀστρακίνοις σκεύεσιν: 4:7)[80] illustrates the fragility of the human body as it undergoes agonizing pain and anguish for the sake of the gospel. This includes "affliction" and all sorts of excruciating tortures (4:8–10).[81] In our sufferings, we are participating in the life and death of Christ, even to the point of carrying the "body of Christ around" (τῷ σώματι) with us (4:10), in order that Jesus' life might be apocalyptically manifested in and by[82] our mortal flesh (4:11). The notion of bodily revelation can only make sense if the scars and wounds of a person are explained by their devotion to Jesus: this verb speaks additionally of "illumination" of the wounds and amplifies the significance of their suffering: that is, the witness of their flesh was a written testimony to their love for Jesus Christ. The contrasts between the "inner" and "outer person" (4:16) does not describe dualism in terms of body and soul, but rather the nature of participation and suffering with Christ. John Goldingay writes with characteristic verve when he says: "If Jesus is magnified in my body, he is magnified in *me* as an essentially embodied person."[83] The body may be destroyed and waste away, but the spirit is at work in renewing our minds and hearts, where we "are being prepared" for glory and power for further good works or for the final resurrection, that which is "eternal" (4:18). In giving up his life, God showed us what life is all about: reflecting the glory of Christ in our lives, living as he lived, loving as he loved, dying as he died—for others and not

---

80. See Lev 6:21; 11:33; 14:50; 15:12 LXX. In each instance of this phrase we see either the frailty of the "jar/s of clay" or the additional comparison with a bowl of bronze (6:21).

81. One is forced to wonder about the severity of these injuries as well, especially in a world where ancient medicine was not known for its stellar reputation.

82. The Greek preposition ἐν can refer to either "in the sphere of" or "by" or "through" in terms of agency. Both meanings are possible here, so I have opted for both in my translation.

83. Goldingay, *Biblical Theology*, 190.

for self. This is the context in which Paul is speaking: sacrificial martyrs awaiting their final vindication at the great day of judgment, and the suffering done by those in Christ is in imitation and in hope of the great day of the resurrection. Jesus' own body, perhaps in a sacramental context, is seen as our own bodies. The body identified as being "mortal," or "frail," as it relates to a lifetime of suffering and abuse and anguish. God has not withheld or hidden himself from us. God is not interested in making himself more glorious, as if such a thing were possible. God is most interested in working in the world to show us how to live and how to please God. God did not see fit to conquer Caesar through violence, or through a raw display of power and sovereignty. Rather God allowed the sovereignties of the world to exercise power over him, to be identified as a slave and to show us the way of life. In giving up his life, God showed us what life is all about: reflecting the glory of Christ in our lives, living as he lived, loving as he loved, dying as he died—for others and not for self.

2.4d: Paul & the Soul

In considering the nature of who a person is, we are left with several perspectives on the theological anthropological composition of a human being. Is she three things (body, soul, and spirit), two things (body and spirit/soul), or one thing (body)? There are various elements of overlap within this debate, as someone could posit that a person is comprised of one thing with multiple aspects (monism). For our purposes, the Christian tradition has seen fit to present three basic options for understanding theological anthropology.

- Trichotomist view—the human person is comprised of three distinct elements: body, soul, and spirit.
- Dichotomist view—the human person is comprised of two distinct elements: body and soul.[84]
- Monistic view—the human person is comprised of one thing: the body.

Physicalism and monism are not equivalent terms, as a monism could affirm the "soul" as an aspect or component of the person. For my purposes,

---

84. This is the view of Cooper, *Body, Soul*.

I will use the term "non-reductive physicalist"[85] to describe my view, although I have found Lynne Rudder Baker's[86] term "constitutionalism" to be quite fascinating: that is, the human person is a material being with no additional distinct components called "soul" or "spirit," at least insofar as they constitute a specific immaterial component of the human person.[87] Simply put, I and other Christians do not believe in the immortal or immaterial "soul." This could also subsumed into what systematic theologian Veli-Matti Kärkkäinen at Fuller Theological Seminary calls "multi-dimensional monism."[88] In any case, much of Paul's anthropological landscape is envisioned in bodily/somatic language and images, and one's view of this question does affect other aspects of Pauline theology, especially in relation to sin and death and the human condition.[89]

Paul uses the Greek word ψυχή ("soul") only thirteen times and in none of these instances do we have a clear reference to what is classically called the immortal or immaterial soul. Consider Romans 2:9: "[there will be] oppression and hardship over every human person (ἐπὶ πᾶσαν ψυχὴν ἀνθρώπου) who produces evil, the Jew first and the Greek."[90] The combination of both "soul" and "human being" illustrates the close relationship between both terms. The verse in context refers to the ones actively "seeking" the things of God who will be given "eternal life:" in 2:7 and in 2:12 we have the language of "perishing, being destroyed" (ἀπολοῦνται). These are verbs that apply to the material embodiment of the human person, and not to an internal factor. The "soul" in context here refers to the human person who will be judged, whether in this world or in the next. Paul confirms this usage later in Romans 11:3 when he invokes the echoing image of Elijah (Rom 11:2) who says to God: "I am left alone, and they are seeking my life

85. See Nancey Murphy, *Bodies and Souls*.

86. Her definition is "I cannot exist without some body that supports certain mental functions," in Baker, "Christian Materialism."

87. Corcoran, a philosopher at Calvin College, puts it well and I echo his work: "notice that by materialism I mean materialism *about* human persons. I do not mean what philosophers mean by *philosophical naturalism*, the claim that what is physical exhausts where there is. Nor do I mean what many non-philosophers mean by materialism, namely, flagrant consumerism and hedonism." *Rethinking*, 13 n2.

88. Kärkkäinen, *Creation and Humanity*. ch. 12.

89. I am limiting myself to Paul specifically as regards the question of monism-dualism, so the question of other writers within the New Testament must be tabled for another discussion.

90. The ESV, argued by some to be a more wooden translation, renders the phrase as I do: "every human person."

(ψυχήν)."⁹¹ Specifically, Paul's intentional echo of 1 Kings 19:10 evokes the imagery of the prophets being "slaughtered" (ἀπέκτειναν), where the life of the human person is in view—not their immaterial soul. The ones who slaughtered the prophets in the First Testament were disinterested in Elijah's spirit but were intent upon his physical death. The "soul" can be killed even. The language of "killing" a "soul" is quite common in the New Testament. Jesus' rhetorical question assumes there is a difference between "saving" or "destroying, slaying" a ψυχὴν in Mark 3:4.⁹² The "death" of the "soul" is also mentioned rather explicitly in Wisdom 1:11 and in Sirach 21:2. This is most evident in Sirach 6:4 where we have the author noting, "the person (ψυχὴ) that does evil will be destroyed (ἀπολεῖ)."

In Romans 13:1, Paul speaks of the human person (ψυχὴ) being "subjected" to the various dominions and authorities, and of Priscilla and Aquila in Romans 16:4 risking their "necks"⁹³ (τράχηλον) for Paul's own "life" (ψυχῆς).⁹⁴ Paul's pervasive bodily imagery coalesces well with the notion of his view of the materiality of the human person. Nothing in Romans—or elsewhere in Paul—suggests that the apostle operated with a body-soul dualism. As is commonly seen, his usage of one of the most common words to mean "soul"⁹⁵—as well as the rest of his uses of this word—reflect normal human bodily life or human existence.⁹⁶ One potential exception that has been offered is Paul's use of the noun in 1 Thessalonians 5:23. This text demands some response, at least to elements within the text that appear problematic from a materialist perspective. Additional interpretive elements concerning sanctification and perfection will be addressed later on.

---

91. First Kgs 19:10–14 LXX.

92. See also the contrast in Matt 10:28: φοβεῖσθε δὲ μᾶλλον τὸν δυνάμενον καὶ ψυχὴν καὶ σῶμα ἀπολέσαι ἐν γεέννῃ.

93. As John Wesley notes "that is, exposed themselves to the utmost danger." Wesley, *New Testament*, 404.

94. The fact that this well-known missionary couple is well known throughout the empire (16:4b) is a powerful testament to the activity of men and women working together.

95. The contrast between "spirit" and "body/flesh" does not prove anthropological dualism: rather it shows a contrast between various states about what it means to be human in certain situations and contexts. The fact that "spirit" and "body/flesh" are dependent upon the other and can be destroyed in an apocalyptic context suggests that vitality or "spiritual life" is involved in the range of meaning of ψυχὴ.

96. 2 Cor 1:23; 12:15; Col 3:23; Eph 6:6; Phil 1:27; 2:30; 1 Thess 2:8.

> "But may he, the God of peace, perfectly sanctify you and may your whole spirit and life (ἡ ψυχὴ) and body be kept blameless by the arrival of our Lord Jesus Christ."

As noted, the use of the "perfect" word here (ὁλοτελής) will be discussed below in chapter 3, so our effort can be more focused on properly interpreting the phrase "whole spirit and life and body" (τὸ πνεῦμα καὶ ἡ ψυχὴ καὶ τὸ σῶμα). I understand the use of ἡ ψυχὴ to be Paul's way of speaking of "life" or "vitality:" or to be more pointed, this is Paul's common understanding of what the word refers to the life or vitality of the human person. For some scholars, this clause refers to gnostic anthropology, although this is doubtful.[97] There are numerous difficulties in accepting this verse as supporting a tripartite vision of anthropology. First, as I believe I have shown above, Paul nowhere speaks like this and so we do not have any direct evidence for this being a new or agreed upon aspect of his theology.[98] Second, it is more likely that Paul is describing one thing rather than three, as each noun can refer to a specific element of the human person without being so distinct as to be a separate entity within the human person. The use of τὸ πνεῦμα throughout 1 Thessalonians almost exclusively appears to refer to the Holy Spirit (1:5–6; 4:8) or the work of the Holy Spirit (5:19). Aside from 1 Thessalonians 2:8 (ψυχὴ: see above), neither of the two other words appears at all in 1 Thessalonians. Thus, we will have to go beyond 1 Thessalonians to understand what Paul specifically means here. However, we can say that the use of the plural pronoun "your" (ὑμῶν) suggests that the entire community is in view, not a singular human person exclusively.[99] One could say that τὸ πνεῦμα refers to the "breath" or "spirit" (=life) of a person, with reference to a bodily perspective of "life" in view (Ezek 18:31; Ps 146:4 LXX). When "the spirit" leaves a person, that person dies, just as the breath leaves their lungs for the last time. Similarly, as we've seen above, Paul's use of ἡ ψυχὴ also refers to a person's mortality and vitality, and this ἡ ψυχὴ likewise can be killed, just as the "body" (τὸ σῶμα): both are finite and subject to the normal course of daily life. It is worth noting that Paul never applies "immortal" or "incorruptible" language to the ψυχὴ. Rather, "what is raised [bodily] is incorruptible/ immortal" (1 Cor 15:42–55) that is, the

---

97. Jewett, *Paul's Anthropological Terms*, 107f.

98. The fact that those who affirm a tripartite anthropology can only appeal to this one text makes it difficult to accept their theological reading of the verse in question.

99. This emphasizes Paul's corporate perspective on the assembly as it relates to election and ecclesiology.

body. All three aspects of this triage of words in the Bible are used to describe mortal, corruptible human beings who can be destroyed, corrupted, or killed—whether by other human beings or by God. Thus, it seems most likely that Paul is referring to the totality of the human person[100] when he speaks of the "wholeness" of sanctification.[101] Accordingly, whatever the "soul" is, it is mortal and it is deeply ingrained into the somatic reality of personhood.[102] To remove the "spirit" or "life" from the "body" only results in the utter and complete cessation of life; hence, humanity is utterly reliant upon God for resurrection, and our bodies are a living testament to God's goodness and kindness in the termination of death and the divine offering of immortality (2 Tim 1:10). Hence, for those who are mired in sin and death, the gospel is a declaration of life, the triumph of God over the final enemy to be annihilated (1 Cor 15:26). The body of Christ is the corporate representation of the individual's corporeal existence. As Susan Eastman has eloquently stated, "the opposite of such fleshly existence is not a dematerialized 'spiritual' life but bodily participation in the 'body of Christ' (Rom 12:4–5; 1 Cor 6:15; 12:12–27)."[103] For Paul, the human person was material, oppressed, violated, enslaved, and in desperate need of liberation. The notion of an immaterial or immortal soul or the escape from the body was not a live option for Paul or his suffering communities. However, the issue is clear: human beings are imperfect, subject to death and corruption, and in desperate need of the glory of God. Without the resurrection of Jesus and our willing participation in his glory, we are dust.

2.4e: Excursus: Aberrant Issues in Paul's Materialist Anthropology?

There are two principal texts in Paul that have been interpreted as supporting a "body/soul" dualism, although a third has sometimes been offered. The first one is found in Philippians 1:20–24 and the other is in 2 Corinthians 5:1–10.[104]

---

100. See Kärkkäinen, *Creation and Humanity*, ch. 12 for a fuller explanation.

101. BWitherington III, *1 and 2 Thessalonians*, 172--73. See also Wanamaker, *Epistles*, 206–7.

102. Matt 10:28.

103. Eastman, *Paul and Person*, 91.

104. Some argue that 1 Thess 4:13–18 is supports anthropological dualism but this confuses the issue of cosmic dualism versus anthropological dualism: 1 Thess 4:13ff is

The context of Philippians 1 is rather straightforward: Paul has spoken of his "chains" or "bonds" (δεσμός) four times in this chapter alone (1:7, 13–14, 17), as well as his "distress" (1:17) and is possibly imprisoned among the Praetorium guard (1:13). Paul desires "deliverance" (σωτηρίαν: 1:19) from this imprisonment, which may result in his death. Given the grotesque spectacle of ancient living conditions in prison, one cannot even begin to imagine the despair and agony Paul felt at being almost entirely alone in this jail—hence we now can see his own reflections in vv. 20–24 below:

> [20]*According to my eager anticipation and hope that in nothing will I be ashamed, but with all boldness as at all times that even now that Christ will be exalted by my body (τῷ σώματί μου), whether through life or through death.* [21]*For me to live is Christ and to die is a "gain."*[105] [22]*But if to live in flesh, this is the fruit*[106] *of my labor, but what I will choose, I do not know.* [23]*But I am distressed by the two, having the desire to die (ἀναλῦσαι)*[107] *and to be with Christ, for that is far greater.* [24]*But to remain in flesh (ἐν τῇ σαρκὶ)*[108] *is necessary for your sakes.*

Throughout, Paul uses metaphorical language to communicate the gravity of his impoverished state, which takes full shape in the so-called Christ hymn in chapter 2 of Philippians. Here, had Paul contrasted σαρκί with ψυχὴ or πνεῦμα, then one might have a case for comparison here. But, unfortunately, the use of σαρκί in both instances simply refers to the human person in a frail and "humiliated" state (Phil 2:3; 3:20–21), as it does in other Jewish texts like Psalms of Solomon 16:13–14: "For if you do not give strength, who can endure discipline in poverty? When a person is tried by his mortality, your testing is in his flesh (ἐν σαρκί), and in the difficulty in

---

about cosmic dualism, not anthropological dualism.

105. This is an economic term, referring to a "profit." Louw-Nida (57.189): "to earn, to gain," that which is gained or earned—"gain, profit." See also BDAG 3669 "a gain, in commercial imagery." This language of "profit" or "gain" is used in the Synoptic Gospels (Matt 16:26 par).

106. "Fruit" (καρπὸς) is used metaphorically to describe the rewards or outcome of Paul's work in the Gospel. The economic or relational transactionalism (1 Cor 9:19–22) is still at work throughout this passage, especially in light of Paul's own need for financial aide (Phil 2:25–30).

107. The aorist infinitive ἀναλῦσαι is being used to communicate Paul's desire to "depart" or to "dissolve," in comparison to being alive. The nature of the contrasts is simple, as we've already seen with Paul, a contrast between death and life.

108. That is, what Paul means is, "to be alive."

poverty." The use of this specific phrase ἐν σαρκί, when seen in context and within the parallels, should press us toward seeing Paul's usage as a simple contrast between life and death, not a metaphysical abstraction about a disembodied state. Tobit 3:6 speaks concerning the duality of "dying" or "living" in difficult trials. It is not entirely accurate to say, "Paul's use of *sōma* strongly suggests that it is a synonym for *sarx*."[109] John Cooper also asserts "there is no mention of a resurrection *sōma* in Philippians 1, which leaves intact the contrast between being in the earthly body and not being embodied at all."[110] This is not at all certain. Paul's primary focus is on union with Christ in the midst of suffering.[111] Furthermore, Paul's description of the "transformation"[112] of our bodies into participatory conformity to Christ's "body of glory" (τῷ σώματι τῆς δόξης) is conditioned upon Christ's return from heaven (3:20). So Cooper has jumped the exegetical gun on this point, as Paul later goes on to show in Philippians 3:20–21.[113] Paul uses similar prepositional phrases in Philippians 3:3–4 (ἐν σαρκί) to describe the nature of circumcision, illustrating the point that they are not "relying on the flesh," which most probably refers to the sphere of human frailty via the image of circumcision. It is an emphasis on the reality of being human: constrained by sin, devolved into imperfection. So, the use of ἐν σαρκί is simply a description of a person who is alive, imprisoned, and desiring to die and be with Christ. The use of the preposition "with" (σὺν: 1:23) in relation to Christ speaks of proximity, intimacy, and anticipation. As Joel Green says, "These are not phrases [with/in Christ in Paul] descriptive of an essentialist

109. Contra Cooper, *Body, Soul*, 167. It must also be said that Cooper does not provide any real exegetical argument to support a dualistic reading of Phil 1:20–24, as his asserted understanding of 2 Cor 5:1–10 is allowed to dictate the contours of the present text.

110. Cooper, *Body, Soul*, 167. It must also be noted that Cooper's charge of "immediate resurrection" to be an "argument from silence" cuts both ways, and so we ought to base our conclusions on inferences derived from exegesis. See *Body, Soul*, 166–67 for this unfortunately polemical charge.

111. "To depart out of bonds, flesh, world, and to be with Christ—in a nearer and fuller union. It is better to depart: it is far better to be with Christ." Wesley, *New Testament*, 507.

112. It must be noted that "transformation" (μετασχηματίσει) is not the same as Cooper's perspective, which is that we "depart" from the flesh in Phil 1:20–24—a reading I believe I have shown to be exegetically unstable. The verb in 3:21 seems to make his reading of 1:20–24 untenable.

113. Cooper's point also about "not being embodied" is also answered by this text, as our "body of humiliation" is "transformed" to be like Christ's, but only at his coming. This assumes we are transformed via resurrection, not disembodied like Cooper argues.

THE IMAGE OF THE UNSEEN GOD

ontology; they do not address issues of *substance*. Rather they express 'my' existence, the persistence of personal identity, in profoundly *relational* terms."[114] The sphere of mortality, corruption, and oppression is countered by being within the sphere of Christ, which is an apocalyptic motif of being "hidden" with Christ (Col 3:1–4) for the great day of resurrection, a day Paul has already obliquely mentioned (Phil 1:6) and is greatly anticipating even if there is some reticence[115] (Phil 3:11). Flesh and blood alone cannot inherit the kingdom of God (1 Cor 15:35–57); the human person needs the Holy Spirit to empower us through the work of Christ and the love of God to bring us into resurrection life. The human person, upon her resurrection, is a body "empowered" by Spirit, but this is not opposed by materiality. Before the resurrection, we are merely human.[116] In the resurrection, we are fully human. Thus, this text is not speaking about departing "from the flesh" in a dualistic or "soulish" sense. The reality of death for Paul was far too prominent and inescapable to him for him to wonder about his "soul" going to heaven. Resurrection is Paul's world, and it is all he has in light of the looming specter of death in that ancient prison. As such, Paul is speaking about the relational disjunction between his present suffering and his hope for future glory, not about anthropological dualism.

The more complex text is in 2 Corinthians 5:1–10, and this requires a substantial amount of unpacking although I believe it is fair to say there are several elements within this text press against a dualistic understanding of anthropology.[117] First, it is widely agreed that Paul's language is quite metaphorical and figurative,[118] so dogmatic assertions need to be tempered with nuance and linguistic precision. To begin with, Paul uses two key verbs to express the idea of addition: the compound "to be clothed" (ἐπενδύομαι:

---

114. Green, *Body, Soul*, 178.

115. The use of the conditional particle εἴ ("if") in 3:11b suggests his lack of certainty, which places a great deal of stress upon Paul's own desire for resurrection in 1:20–24.

116. The Adamic reality of Rom 7:7–25 is immediately applicable to this idea, especially as it relates to claims that try to press Paul towards a sense of anthropological dualism. However, the embodied nature of Paul's metaphoric language in Rom 7:7–25 is not contingent upon the release of the soul from the body, but the deliverance of the body from condemnation (Rom 8:1).

117. A view, oddly, that Cooper himself ultimately does not really argue for in vv. 1–5. See *Body, Soul*, 159.

118. A point rightly noted by Cooper, *Body, Soul*, 156–57, although he does go on to charge a certain school of interpretation with being able only "to explain [this text] away." Such a claim is superfluous as the quest for scriptural hegemony is a perilous affair that affects us all.

also in v. 4) as well as the more common verb "to clothe" (ἐνδύω: v. 3). This verb is used throughout the Pauline corpus to refer to "putting on" metaphorical armor (Rom 13:12; Eph 6:11–14; 1 Thess 5:8) and to "putting on" Christ himself (Rom 13:14) as opposed to evil desires (Col 3:10–12); this suggests that the addition of Christ to a person's spiritual framework results in a changed ethical outlook: Christ is the north star to our journey, for without him we are bound to stumble in the dark. Similarly, and perhaps most importantly, Paul uses this verb in 1 Cor 15:53–54 to speak of "putting on" (ἐνδύω) imperishability and immortality, where the comparison is between mortal/corruptible bodies and the apocalyptic reality of eternal life and bodily resurrection. Paul also speaks of people within the eschatological community of "putting on Christ" in reference to baptism (Gal 3:27). In each instance, Paul appears to refer to a sphere of influence (Christ, immortality, etc.), and this can be a protective placement like armor, at least in terms of analogy or metaphor. The verb can reflect a change of status according to baptism (Gal 3:27), but it remains difficult to see any notion of anthropological dualism at play with Paul's use of the verb. In every instance, the body (either as the somatic reality of the human person or the ethical conduct of the human person) is in view, and so it is not tenable to claim that the verb might refer to "the naked self rather than over the earthly body."[119] In Tobit 1:17, the author speaks of a person being "naked" and within the same verse speaks of a corpse being outside the city, suggesting some correspondence between death and "nakedness." For Paul, most likely the "nakedness" *is* the "body," not the inner self. The use of the word does not appear to refer to the "soul" in the Second Temple literature in any metaphorical way, "wherein to be found 'naked' was to suffer humiliation, and to lose one's status as a human."[120] The final issue of "dualism" is found in the use of the verb "to be away, depart" (ἐκδημέω) in 1 Corinthians 5:6–9. But upon closer examination, 5:6 proves rather decisive for a physicalist understanding: to be embodied is to be, in some sense, away from God.[121] To be "at home in the body" is to be alive, marked with mortality and frailty and the inevitability of death. Yet Paul's victorious cry despite his anguish is saturated with confidence. Because he knows about the distinction between being presently human and still away from God, where faithfulness plays a

---

119. Per Cooper, *Body, Soul*, 157.

120. Green, *Body, Soul*, 171.

121. Father, Son and Spirit are all mentioned in 2 Cor 5:5–6, which suggests Paul's Trinitarian theology is at play within resurrection.

decisive factor in his union with Christ (5:7). Even though to be "away from the body" (that is, his current body of humiliation and persecution) is to be with Christ, and "home" with the Lord is "pleasing," Paul's ultimate conclusion is that in either life or death, Christ's life might be manifested to others. The entire pericope is focused upon the humiliation of death and decay, which is contrasted with apocalyptic hope and the power of the resurrection. The fact that the body (i.e., the person) is held to account for their good or sinful deeds (5:10) reflects the somatic nature of Pauline ethics and the reality of the material and frail condition that humanity is within. The sequence is rather simple: the "present evil age" (Gal 1:4) reflects the totality of human existence as cruel, unusual, frail, and barbaric. Paul's reference throughout to the "tent" and "building" are metaphors for speaking of the resurrection of the body, the body empowered by the Holy Spirit. The importance of Paul's materialism in reference to Christian perfection is this: the material world is enslaved and subject to decay and brutality—far from perfection! What distinguishes this from Gnosticism (where the flesh is irrelevant) is the belief that the transformation of the whole person (body and mind) begins with the body. Bodily perfection can only be actualized in the resurrection, but the renewing of our minds and hearts toward perfect holiness begins now. The perfection of Christ's body in glorification is the hope of our present circumstances, and we both hope and pray for the restoration of who we are into what we were meant to be—sanctification unto perfection—only the perfect Son can accomplish that.

2.4f: The Triune God & the Human Condition: A Short Summarization

There is a certain curiosity about Paul's view of the human person, insofar as his view speaks highly of the human capacity to act freely without compulsion: whether it is through the slave owner freely responding to Onesimus (Philemon vv. 12–14), Jews and the people of the nations acting in morally responsible or irresponsible ways (Rom 9:30–32),[122] or any exercise of faithfulness (Rom 1:16; 4:4–5: 6:8). Specifically, Christ's own faithfulness to God (Rom 3:22; Gal 3:22) is paradigmatic for the human person's free and faithful participation in Christ's faithfulness (Gal 2:16). Christ-faith is the needed paradigm for those seeking the kindness of God. Paul's use of

---

122. For a persuasive reading that largely mirrors my own reading and places Rom 9 (and Paul specifically) within a Jewish context, see Thornhill, *Chosen People*.

this faith/allegiance language, indeed his very point in Galatians, concerns the work of the eternal Son who was faithful (i.e., "humble") to his very end so that we "might profess allegiance to/in Christ Jesus" (εἰς Χριστὸν Ἰησοῦν ἐπιστεύσαμεν: Gal 2:16b). In accordance with the subjective genitive reading, we see that the initial cause of rectification[123] is always centered on the activity of the Son, and the subsequent synergistic response of the human person is enacted in faithful allegiance to the Son. Galatians 2:16 breaks down as follows:

> 2:16a: Rectification is brought forth by the faithful life of Jesus (Jesus as source).
> 2:16b: Rectification is enacted by human participation in faith to Jesus.
> 2:16c: So that humanity might be rectified by Jesus' faithfulness.

The human response to such faith is imitation and participation, in "seeking to be rectified in/by Christ" (Gal 2:17a), where such a state can only be achieved by means of the work of the Son. Therefore, the faithfulness of the Son is our faithfulness. The faithfulness of Jesus is the conclusive model for our own participation in suffering and perfection. This becomes our call to suffer, live, and die. Jesus' humanness (1 Tim 2:4–6 and Rom 5:12–21ff in their use of the generic ἄνθρωπος to describe Jesus) is central to this case, as the Son is never spoken of being "obedient" or "subordinate" before his incarnation.[124] Indeed, because of the Son's faithfulness, we can now "enjoy peace with God" (Rom 5:1).[125] The humanity of the Son as the one who took on "sinful human flesh" (ὁμοιώματι σαρκὸς ἁμαρτίας) suggests that the realm of sin and death was dealt a deathblow by the bodily presence of Jesus of Nazareth, where the war between perfection and utter depravity was ceased: "we with our sinful flesh were devoted to death. But God sending his own Son in the likeness of that flesh, though pure from sin, he condemned that sin[126] which was in our flesh: gave sentence that sin

---

123. Often this word is translated as "justification," but the verbal form δικαιόω (used in all three clauses) most likely refers to the "making of something right," or "rectification."

124. This is a point Heb 5:8 makes rather forcefully. Obedience was not an ontological or functional status for the Son: rather, it was a self-chosen state of humiliation for our glorification and ultimate rectification.

125. This reading (that is, the subjunctive) should be adopted due to the superior textual evidence (ℵ* A B* C D K L 33) and the rhetorical structure. See Porter, "Argument of Romans," 655–77 and adopted by Jewett, *Romans*, 344.

126. Wesley rightly points out that God did not condemn Jesus, but rather sin. Thus, while the element of substitution or exchange is deeply woven in the fabric of this text,

should be destroyed,[127] and the believer wholly delivered from it."[128] The synergistic model of God's work and human participation runs throughout Paul without pause or stipulation (Eph 1:19; Phil 2:12–13), which is only in accordance with the calling of the Spirit (Gal 5:16–17).[129] The language of "seeking," especially when used in the active tense form, refers to an agent actively engaged in the process of examining or pursuing someone or something. For example, love does not "seek itself" (1 Cor 13:5). Indeed, because of Christ's own life of faithfulness, we can be among those who are "seeking to be rectified in Christ!" (ζητοῦντες δικαιωθῆναι ἐν Χριστῷ: Gal 2:17a), where even the death of Christ is displayed as being the antidote to sin and enslavement: we live for Christ because Christ died for us (Gal 2:20). The fact that Paul goes to endless pains to explain how Christ is uninvolved personally with sin illustrates the point of the sinlessness of Christ in relation to his incarnation. Christ cannot be a slave to sin, and we are freed from the sovereignty of sin (Rom 6:4). The preexistent Son is at the center of all reality and hence is our guiding light as we talk about sanctification. As Christ came into the world perfect and without sin, so too we will also be perfected into the image of Christ by the Holy Spirit.

2.4g: Human Freedom & Christ

Paul's model of human participation in Christ assumes that human beings are free to do so, just as the eternal Son freely and actively "took the form of a slave" (Phil 2:6–7). For those who "accept the gift of righteousness with reign in eternal life" (Rom 5:17) and those who "purify themselves" will be "sanctified" (2 Tim 2:21),[130] there is life. More specifically, the active participle (λαβών: taking "the form") in Philippians 2 refers to an active agent performing a specific action: the Son "accepted/took" the form of a slave, and human beings are told to have this same "mindset" (Phil

---

the penal or retributive aspect of such atonement theories remains curiously absent.

127. 1 Cor 15:20–28, where it is death that is ultimately annihilated. This pericope will be discussed in detail throughout the rest of this book.

128. Wesley, *Explanatory Notes*, 381.

129. For my Reformed sisters and brothers who might enjoy an intriguing defense of "Libertarian Calvinism" by a leading Reformed theologian (and my former professor), see Crisp, *Deviant Calvinism*, ch. 3.

130. This text will be explored below in more detail.

2:5a).¹³¹ This assumes agency and capacity on the part of human kind in our response to Christ.¹³² The human person, despite her state of frailty and sinfulness, is nonetheless called upon to participate in the vocation of God despite her circumstances. We are called toward perfection in Christ, the abolition of our sinful desires. Christ's perfection in his incarnate and resurrection state is a calling for us to live a life that brings pleasure to God and brings goodness to our neighbors, where our lives are marked as active "co-workers" (συνεργός)¹³³ of God (1 Cor 3:9; 1 Thess 3:2; perhaps Rom 8:28)¹³⁴ in the gospel, where even the corporate nature of the body of Christ is mentioned.¹³⁵ Every time Paul uses the word συνεργός, the reference concerns active agents participating together in a common goal, most often in working together for the gospel (Rom 16:3, 9, 21) and together in missional activity (2 Cor 1:24; 8:23; Phil 2:25; 4:3; Col 4:11; Philemon 1, 24). Hence, terms like "free will" or "human participation" or "synergism" are appropriate to describe Paul's vision of humanity working in collaboration with God and others (1 Macc 12:1; 2 Macc 8:7; 14:5). Paul is quite clear about the cooperative work done by God and humanity together in 2 Corinthians 6:1:

> Working together (συνεργοῦντες) we also exhort you to not welcome the favor of God in vain.

Simply put, Paul believed that the human person was free to respond or reject God's gracious gift of Christ and participate in union with Christ by the empowerment of the Holy Spirit.¹³⁶ Because of Christ's willingness to

---

131. More pointedly, the Greek verb φρονέω can often suggest a manner of living, or a lifestyle oriented around the ethical life, and in this case that would reflect the calling of Christ.

132. For insightful books that I find remarkably compelling that explore the Bible's view of love and freedom, see Peckham, *Theodicy of Love* and *Love of God*.

133. See the use in 1 Esd 7:2 in reference to priests and elders "working together."

134. "We know that all things cooperate together for those who love God." Paul's use of the verbal form συνεργεῖ in Rom 8:28 most likely refers to God "working with, cooperating with" all things "for good." It is most likely that Paul has synergism in mind, as Jewett, *Romans*, 527–28 and n.211 has shown. See also Thornhill, *Chosen People*, 230–32. The human action of loving God is a free response to God's sovereign goodness, which works best within a synergistic system or model. See the powerful arguments by Haley Goranson Jacob, *Conformed to Image*.

135. 1 Cor 3:9b: "you are God's building" and "you are God's temple" in 3:17b.

136. For an excellent philosophical work that surveys this question with eloquence and persuasive power, see Timpe, *Free Will*. My thanks to Dr. Jerry L. Walls of Houston Baptist University for recommending this resource to me.

impoverish himself on our behalf, we are willing to participate in the calling of God through him. This free action (Christ's self-impoverishment) is an act freely taken and freely assumed, removing any notion of hierarchy or "tier" between the Father and the Son.[137] Additionally, the Christ-gift (2 Cor 8:9) assumes human co-operation with Christ and those who accept his intercession: a gift given to a person requires active participation in concert with what has been given. Such a gift compels but does not force or exact deterministic pressure upon the opposing party.

Despite our sinful status and our enslavement to the various powers and one another, Paul nevertheless affirmed our cooperative activity with God through the means of the liberating power of the Holy Spirit in grace. The materiality of Christ's glorified body is coordinate with Paul's anthropology, and the resurrection of Jesus has profound implication for how the church relates to Christ in terms of sanctification. How does Christ's activity in atonement and liberation promote our journey toward holiness? What did Paul believe about the nature of holiness? With Paul's Christology and anthropology explored, at least in a cursory fashion, we now turn to sanctification and the process by which a human person is rectified before God—the very heart of this book.[138]

---

137. For more on this point, see Butner's work above as well as the recent volume edited by Bird and Harrower, *Trinity*.

138. My special thanks to my friends Dr. Johnathan Pritchett and Dr. Braxton Hunter of Trinity College of the Bible and Theological Seminary for their frequent conversations concerning Christian materialism and dualism: hopefully the labors of those extended conversations yield some fruit within this chapter.

3

The Perfection of Our Faithful Wills

Paul's Apocalyptic Vision

3.1: Initial Renewal: Demarcations & Clarifications Concerning Holiness

I remember sitting in a seminary class with a guy named Chad. Chad came from a background of drugs and for a time was living homeless in Northern California, and we started talking about his life and journey toward God. He had an encounter with the Holy Spirit and, by the miraculous grace of God, the desire and addiction to drugs were removed entirely from his life. For most of us, this sort of inexplicable change does not happen. Renewal or the process of sanctification is more often a journey with a body of believers in the presence of the Holy Spirit. The nature of Pauline sanctification or holiness is this: the active outworking of a person to imitate the life lived by Jesus of Nazareth. This implies the utter rejection of sin and the active lifestyle of holiness in relation to neighborly love and divine glorification. Holiness is the refusal to participate in what God has deemed as sinful and destructive. Holiness is love for God and love for nothing else outside of God.

What makes these sorts of diverse experiences unique and complex is that Paul's language of "renewal" (ἀνακαίνωσις) tells us that "perfection" affects the totality of the human person and her "mind" (νοῦς; Eph 4:23): the entire person is to be included in "renewal," and the process of sanctification or holiness is rarely if ever instantaneous. "That is why we do not lose heart, but even if our outer humanity is being utterly corrupted, yet our innerness is being renewed day by day" (2 Cor 4:16). Therefore, the transforming power of the gift of Christ (Eph 4:7) affects the totality of the human person in her life lived in faithful pursuit of God's vocation for her. This is also connected to Christ being the "image of God" (2 Cor 4:4; Col 1:15–20), who calls us to be his brothers and sisters. The human person is in desperate need of "emancipation" (ἀπολύτρωσις) and this emancipation includes her entire person (Rom 8:23). In the triadic clause following the prepositional conclusion in 1 Corinthians 1:30, we have "rectification and sanctification and emancipation" (δικαιοσύνη τε καὶ ἁγιασμὸς καὶ ἀπολύτρωσις) as finding their source "from God" (ἀπὸ θεοῦ). The significance of this is exemplified in the linking together of three distinct nouns that follow from the giving of "wisdom." The initiation of perfection begins with Christ as the gift from God to us for our present and future perfection. Thus, rectification, holiness, and Godly emancipation are thematically linked to the work of God in our lives as well as our faithful pursuit of what God desires for us. If the Holy Spirit is determined to instantly sanctify us, then who can stop the Spirit? If the Holy Spirit desires to journey with us through our sufferings and agonies, then who will cast the Holy Spirit away? As John Wesley said, "one perfected in love may grow in grace far swifter than he did before."[1] Perfection by the power of the Holy Spirit is contagious for those seeking the reckless love of God.

3.2: Perfecting Holiness: Biblical Theology & Paul's Vision of Perfection

When speaking of "perfection," Paul almost always uses a specific word: the noun τέλος and the verbal form τελέω (along with various compounds like ἐπιτελέω). Space does not permit us to explore all of Paul's uses of this complex word group, but it is sufficient to note that the word has a wide semantic range. Some lexicons like Liddel-Scott (LS 42313) gloss this term as "the fulfillment or completion of anything." Other lexicons such as

---

1. Cited in Collins, *Theology*, 294.

BDAG 6342 render the term as "a point in time that marks culmination, end, outcome." In other instances, the word clearly refers to a tax of some sort (Rom 13:7). In the following chapter, we will focus on various Pauline Epistles where this word occurs with the other word group for "holiness" or "sanctification,"[2] with specific reference to the τέλος word group if need be.[3] We will see that the glory of God is manifested in perfection, especially in how Paul describes the struggles of life and sinful people in light of the Holy Spirit's call toward perfection in their forsaking of sin. God is most glorified when we become most like him, where sin is cleansed, and we are united fully to the Godhead in glory and honor and immortality.

The structure of this chapter is relatively straightforward. There are certain key phrases in Paul's letters that rather explicitly support the doctrine of entire sanctification, while other texts and concepts imply such a doctrine. As is the case when dealing with dogmatic theology, one is forced to consider both the historical particularities of the ancient world and the concerns of Christian theology in our present age. For me, interpreting these historical texts theologically has pressed me to consider the various aspects of how the human person can be entirely sanctified in this life.

Perhaps the best initial text is found in Romans 6:6. For Wesleyans—and, indeed, all Christians—we are deeply and profoundly aware of who we are as creatures. Paul captures this rather poignantly when he writes, "Knowing this, that our old self was crucified along with him for the purpose of bringing the body of Sin to utter nothingness (καταργηθῇ) so that we would no longer be enslaved to Sin" (Rom 6:6). As we noted earlier, Paul's Christology and his doctrine of humanity are intertwined here; as Wesley says, "This, in a believer, is crucified with Christ, mortified, gradually

---

2. BDAG 47 defines ἁγιωσύνη as "state of being in accord with divine standards of virtue." Similarly, in BDAG 43, the verbal form is defined as "set apart into the realm of the sacred." The aspect of holiness or sanctification are therefore appropriate renderings of this word group, and there is far less complexity concerning the variegated meanings.

3. The τέλος word group occurs through the majority of the Pauline literature, sometimes in conjunction with the "Law." Beginning in Rom 2:27, we have a reference to "the one keeping/fulfilling the Law" (τὸν νόμον τελοῦσα) in reference to the debate over the place of the people of the nations (=so-called gentiles) in the church. The participle τελοῦσα suggests an active fulfillment on the part of the person persisting or actively engaging with the Law, and this person will have judgment rights over the Jew. Whereas the person of the nations, though uncircumcised, has been faithful to God's Law, the Jew has not. Thus, the participle fits well with Paul's axiom of faithfulness on the part of an active agent, and their complete fulfillment of the requirements of the Law (at least hypothetically).

THE PERFECTION OF OUR FAITHFUL WILLS

killed, by virtue of our union with him."[4] Sin, in whatever form, is utterly removed from the life of a believer—this results in the interchange between enslavement and emancipation. The believer is no longer subjected nor guided by the power of sin and death. As the "body of Sin" is brought to utter nothingness, so too will the various "powers" and "sovereignties" (1 Cor 2:6; 15:24–26) be brought to utter nothingness. This notion of sin being a force to be utterly removed is reflected in 2 Maccabees 12:42: "and they turned toward prayer that the sin that had been made would be utterly and completely (τελείως) removed." The perfective aspect of faith is also seen in Sirach 34:8: "without lies the law will be fully accomplished and wisdom is perfected (τελείωσις) in the mouth of the faithful one (πιστῷ)."[5] This *telos* word group occurs often throughout the LXX in a context of sacrifice and the rectification of the community in relation to God.[6] Sin, as an operative force, is a reality that must be resisted, and *can* be resisted, as it is no longer able to operate in the space the Holy Spirit has claimed. The interrelation of "eternal life" and "holiness" (Rom 6:19–22) illustrates the necessary association Paul makes between apocalyptic life and the perfective accumulation of the ethical life. Our lives are apocalyptic examples of Christ's own life, and our hope for "eternal life" is predicated upon faithfulness to Christ, forsaking the things of death and destruction for the living God.

Two other passages in Romans deserve some specific exegesis. Both Romans 12:1–2 and Romans 15:16 are thematically linked together.[7] Romans 12:1–2: "And do not be conformed to this age, but transform yourselves[8] in the renewing of your mind, for you to test yourselves about what the will of God is: what is good and well-pleasing and perfect (τέλειον)." In a context of personal reflection, the pursuit of God's will and desire for us as people of faith is summed up in the triadic form: good and well-pleasing and perfect. All three aspects of "testing" or "discerning" on our part cannot be summed up in a single word—rather, all three words describe the emotional and corporate responsibility we have toward one another: we

---

4. Wesley, *Explanatory Notes*, 377.

5. That is, the faithfulness of a person or a community is co-operative in how the ethics of the person of God are lived out. That is, the honest adherence of a community to God's law results in the "perfection of wisdom."

6. Exod 29:1–35.

7. Jewett, *Romans*, 729.

8. The imperatival form of this word suggests a free action on the part of the agent performing the verb: that is, the human person. The middle/passive element corresponds to God's initiation and the imperative is our free response in participation.

are to be good to our brothers, sisters, neighbors, and enemies; we are to be well-pleasing to God by these things; we are to be perfect in pursuing and striving toward what God has called us to be. The image of "perfect" here is not a far-off goal reserved for people with excellent testimonies or exciting stories about a life no longer lived in sexual immorality, anger, or drug abuse. Rather, the idea of "perfect" in Romans 12:1–2 is that renunciation of sin and "testing" God's demands in order to discern our vocation in God's kingdom. Our transformation is not to be done in an isolated fashion: rather, we need the Holy Spirit working through the body of believers around us.[9] The emphasis on "bodies" is Paul's way of stressing our actions and mindset as embodied creatures under the reign of the Spirit. The utter transformation of our personhood by the desire of God is precisely what Paul is saying. The goal is not conformity to Greco-Roman ideals or our modern-day notions of nationalism but faithful allegiance to Jesus Christ and to Jesus Christ alone.

The pneumatic element of sanctification is especially present toward the end of Romans where Paul speaks about the people of the nations being "sanctified by the Holy Spirit" (Rom 15:6). The verb here for sanctification is ἡγιασμένη (perfect tense form), and this verb is used to describe what is called a "complete and undifferentiated process,"[10] where the people of the nations are entirely set apart in terms of holiness, and this is done by means of the Holy Spirit and within the sphere of the Spirit.[11] As Jewett remarks, "It is the transformation of their social life that requires the appellation 'holy.'"[12] Paul's own "priestly service"[13] (Rom 15:6a) is for Christ Jesus and for the gospel of God. Hence, even before we've moved from Romans in our study, we can see the Trinitarian force of sanctification in Paul's thought—especially as it relates to the perfective aspect of people being included in

---

9. This corporate body of faithful people may be the local church, a Bible study, or a group of friends who fellowship together. Whatever the case may be, do not forsake one another for yourselves.

10. Porter, *Idioms*, 21. To be clear, I am not claiming that the "perfect tense form" is what "perfection" means.

11. Fee notes, "One cannot tell whether Paul intends it to be instrumental or locative of sphere." As I have rendered and exegeted the phrase, I suspect both understandings are true, but the instrumental nature of the dative case would result, by consequence, in the locative sphere of the Spirit's presence. Fee, *Empowering Presence*, 626 n.459.

12. Jewett, *Romans*, 908.

13. This word does not refer simply to "ministry" in the sense that the ESV renders it; rather, in context the word refers to cultic or priestly works done in a temple setting.

God's family. While this verse may speak about their "separateness"[14] from the rest of the nations, this does not explain the full force of Paul's Trinitarian work here: the nations are an "offering" (προσφορὰ)[15] to the triune God, a free offering that cannot be blemished or stained by pagan activities or woefully sinful impulses. Similarly, the Holy Spirit is involved in "love" (Rom 5:5), intercession (Rom 8:27), testifying (Rom 9:1), and the attributes of the kingdom of God: rectification, peace, joy, and especially hope for those who are hopeless (Rom 14:17; 15:13).

In essence, Romans 15:16 (along with other texts) recapitulates Paul's entire argument from Romans 9–11 in that the people of the nations and the Jewish people are both sanctified and holy people, regardless of geography, gender, or social status—the oneness of the body of Christ does not show privilege or preference toward those whom God calls "sons" and "daughters." Temporal election or calling for vocational purposes does not result in favoritism for those who were initially not called by God.[16] Paul has moved the holiness of the people out of the confines of the temple and granted it to every Jew and to all of the people of the nations who exercise faithful allegiance to King Jesus; in his priestly service to God and Christ, Paul has brought the people of the nations near, for the purpose of their being made holy by God. This aligns perfectly with Romans 11:32–36, where Paul's climactic cry is the universal triumph of God's ultimate gratuitous display of mercy.[17] All of humanity's sins—whether personal, corporate, or systemic—are undermined by God's severe and generous mercy toward those who are most in need of his favor and kindness. Sanctification, in Romans, is the work of the Holy Spirit in coordination with Christology—the one who summarizes all things in him and is the τέλος of our calling to be a righteous and perfect people, steeped in holiness and fully united to the will of God-in-Christ. Hence, the doctrine of entire sanctification plays an integral part in the theology of Romans as it relates to how Christians pursue holiness despite the influence of Rome and sin.

The conflict in Corinth spans at least two Epistles, with at least one Epistle not surviving. Given the extraordinary conflict between Paul and

---

14. If one adopts a wooden reading of the word in question, of course.
15. Odes 7:38; Sirach 34:18; 35:5; 46:16; 50:13.
16. Thornhill, *Chosen People*, 229–53.
17. Longenecker puts it this way: "the apostle declares that undergirding the entire course of God's salvation history—is God's desire to 'have mercy on them all' (i.e. on all people, whatever their ethnic heritage, their geographical location, and their particular situation or circumstance)." *Epistle to Romans*, 902.

the various apostolic groups and schismatic factions, it is striking that the apostle begins 1 Corinthians 1:2 with him writing "to the assembly of God, sanctified (ἡγιασμένοις) in[18] Christ Jesus who are in Corinth[19] called saints, with everyone who is calling on the name of our Lord Jesus Christ in every place: theirs and even ours." What is compelling about this brief opening is that Paul does not believe the Corinthian church has been entirely sanctified, so there is an element of sarcasm here (1:10–11 per "divisions" and "dissentions"). Nevertheless, the lack of perfection does not diminish the rather obvious call toward perfection. Indeed, the power of Christ is involved here as Christ "will strengthen" the church to the "end" (τέλους), the "day of our Lord Jesus Christ" (1:8).[20] Not only this, Christ will make us "blameless," a state only worked out through the sphere of Christ's presence and influence. Those who are called "holy ones" (ἁγίοις)[21] are described as ones who are "called" (κλητοῖς); more specifically, the ones who were beckoned and welcomed by God to be "holy" are the ones who have partaken of the Son's work. Both Gordon Fee and Anthony Thiselton spar about the nature of the "verdict of God" and the "blameless behavior."[22] However, one should not push both ideas apart. The human response[23] to God's declaration of emancipation (1:30) clearly has ethical implications, as we will discuss later. Both 1 Corinthians 1:2 and 1:8 present us with the principal idea of rectification in Christ Jesus, and this universal scope where everyone who "calls upon" Christ will be rectified as an "emancipated" (1:30) holy one of God. The presence and person of Christ is the principal source of our own "rectification, sanctification, and emancipation" (δικαιοσύνη τε καὶ ἁγιασμὸς καὶ ἀπολύτρωσις). These attributes, including wisdom, "belong

---

18. The locative meaning ("in") of this preposition does not exclude agency. It is "in" Christ and "through" Christ that sanctification occurs.

19. There is a textual variant here: some early witnesses (01 Sinaiticus; 02 A Alexandrinus) have the phrase "those being in Corinth" before the phrase "sanctified." However, the earliest extant witness we have (P46 B) has the sentence in the order I have translated, so I believe this is the best reading.

20. This phrase clearly has an apocalyptic outlook, as the phrase "day of the Lord" indicates.

21. See also 1 Cor 14:33; 16:1, 15, 20; 2 Cor 1:1; 8:4; 9:1, 12; 13:12.

22. See Thiselton, *First Epistle*, 102.

23. Specifically, "all who call upon" (πᾶσιν τοῖς ἐπικαλουμένοις) the name of the Lord (1:2b) suggests the active desire of people to be united to Christ in the exercise of their free will.

together, and both characterize Christ"[24] and are constituted by Christ's saving activity in the cosmos. The activity of God-in-Christ confers what might be called the great transference, from one reality to another. In contrast to worldly wisdom, we have Christ, who is our rectification, and the imagery of a "holy" (ἁγιασμὸς) temple[25] suggests a reality without sin in the presence of God (1 Cor 3:17).[26]

In 1 Corinthians 2:6, Paul asserts "but among the 'perfected ones' (τελείοις) we speak wisdom, but it is not the wisdom of this world order nor the rulers of this world order[27] being utterly destroyed (καταργουμένων)."[28] Similar to his use of τοῦ αἰῶνος, Paul is perhaps anticipating the final annihilation of the sovereignties in 1 Corinthians 15:24, and the use of this participle suggests that this is a phase that has begun. Hence, even though they exercise dominion at the current time, their time of annihilation is immanent. Here, Paul is indulging in some sarcasm, as it is likely the Corinthian church has drunk deeply from the postmodern well. The logic is rather stark: those who do not have the "mind of Christ" (2:16) or the ethical impulses of the Spirit (6:1–20; ch.7) are sarcastically compared to those who are "perfect." Rather, this is an assertion about absurd self-promotion, where the flight of human narcissism has risen to disparate heights of indulgence. Sanctification remains a telic ideal, and the lack of present perfection in terms of holiness does not mitigate Paul's ultimate desire for ethical holiness in his communities and in our communities as well. Far from it! The ones who have been entirely sanctified are contrasted with the current world order; this world order is bound over to destruction.[29]

Paul uses several key nouns and verbs in 1 Corinthians ch.6–7. He refers to the people he's addressing as "saints" or "holy ones" (6:1–2, 19; 7:34: ἅγιος) in relation to their troubling behavior concerning lawsuits. This entire display of the rich taking the poor to court is "shameful" (ἐντροπὴν: 6:5), and the lack of communal mutuality is placing the assembly at great

---

24. Thiselton, *First Epistle*, 191.

25. The temple in 1 Cor 3:15–17 is the body of Christ, the community of believers.

26. Indeed, the utter abolition of evil remains one of Paul's more central apocalyptic themes. The exercise of divine or secular sovereignty cannot co-exist with a God of holy love. Hence, the fall of the sovereignties remains certain. This will be talked about later.

27. Paul's use of τοῦ αἰῶνος suggests both the element of time (the present reality or age) and the negative aspect of being under evil sovereignties: hence, my translations.

28. For a discussion about whether these are spiritual or secular powers (I believe they are both), see Thiselton, *First Epistle*, 238–39.

29. Hays, *First Corinthians*, 43.

risk. The wealthy members are wielding authority over the weak ones, and Paul's response is to severely criticize the people in positions of actualized power (6:9–10) with a stringent vice-list that indicts everyone. But as John Wesley pointed out, "we may learn that we are never secure from the greatest sins."[30] Paul's rather cutting response to various people is to remind them of the work of God-in-Christ-through-the-Holy-Spirit in 6:11: "and such were[31] some of you: but you washed, but you were sanctified (ἡγιάσθητε), but you were rectified (ἐδικαιώθητε) in the name of the Lord Jesus and by the Spirit of our God."[32] When Paul speaks additionally of marriage in 1 Corinthians 7:1–16, he highlights the mutual sanctification at play in marriage between husband and wife (7:14): "for the unbelieving husband is sanctified by the wife, and the unbelieving wife is sanctified by the husband: therefore, your[33] children would be unclean, but now they are holy." The perfect tense form of the verb ἡγίασται ("to sanctify") is exactly parallel between husband and wife, and Paul's thoroughly radical egalitarian contention is that both genders are agents of virtue and sanctification within marriage, and the holiness involved renders them as united to Christ. Throughout 1 Corinthians 6–7 we see the various aspects of marital sex within Paul's context as it relates to how women and men interact in marriage by the empowerment of the Holy Spirit and in prophecy.[34] Hence, while 1 Corinthians contains a great deal of sarcasm and rhetorical bite, Paul's goal is the unity of a fractious church.

In 2 Corinthians, however, Paul's general outlook is one of combative despair over the conflict within his various assemblies that has bubbled over the cauldron; his goal is ultimately reconciliation despite the schisms that have erupted.[35] Hence, "holiness" and "sanctification" have ceased to

---

30. Wesley, *Explanatory Notes*, 419.

31. The being verb "were" (ἦτε) refers to a past status or persona, where the desire for sexual immorality and economic exploitation are removed.

32. All three verbs involved are in the aorist tense form, signifying an act that has transferred or removed those formerly identified by this vice list and placed them into the sanctifying presence of Christ and the Spirit of God.

33. The plural form of this pronoun refers to husband and wife in relation to marital sanctification, and we will discuss its importance in ch. 4.

34. 1 Cor 14:20: "Brothers and sisters, do not be children in your mindset. But in evil [you] act as infants, but in your mindset be perfect (τέλειοι)." See also 1 Cor 13:10. The contrast between evil actions/ways of thinking is seen in contrast with the "perfect," where the vision of holy love eradicates the necessity for evil and the desire for sinfulness.

35. Witherington III, *Conflict and Community*, 327–28.

be about sex and marriage as in 1 Corinthians, and Paul's second letter to the "saints"[36] in Corinth has a different emphasis. That is, Paul and his various co-workers have endured immense suffering and persecution for the gospel. In 2 Corinthians 6:4–6 Paul lays this out rather plainly:

> "But in all things we demonstrate ourselves as God's ministers: by great perseverance, by afflictions, by hardships, by anguishing moments, by floggings, by imprisonments, by riots, by difficult work, by lack of sleep, by famishment: in purity, in knowledge, in forbearance, in kindness—by the Holy Spirit in unpretentious love!"

Similarly, the witness of the various apostles in 2 Corinthians 1:12 is said to be "in a lifestyle of holiness (ἁγιότητι) and sincerity for God, not in earthly wisdom." In both texts, we have the immanence of love as set above all manner of oppression and degradation, without pause or stammer. The life lived in holiness and sanctification is said to reflect "sincerity for God" and a love that lacks pretense and hypocrisy (6:6). The impact of entire sanctification presses upon us the value and necessity of seeking "unpretentious love" despite trials and agonies, where the thought of resistance to the various gods, empires, and idols becomes encompassed in a boast of the loving-kindness of the triune God. However, there is a problem: why has the Holy Spirit been included in a list of human virtues in 6:6? I suspect the answer is twofold. First, the use of the preposition ἐν ("in" or "by") most likely includes the notion of agency, and thus it should be understood as "by the Holy Spirit." Second, it is not uncommon for Paul to include the Spirit in a discourse on ethical practice (Gal 5:18–23). The Holy Spirit, as the one who guides and empowers the community of faith, is a fitting inclusion to the end of Paul's sentence especially as it relates to unpretentious love. It is because of all these things in these few verses that Paul can assert the following in 2 Corinthians 12:9:

> And he has said to me, "My gracious favor is sufficient for you, for power is made perfect (τελεῖται) by weakness"—most gladly there will I boast even more in my weakness so that the power of Christ will dwell in me.

True power for Paul lies not in physical might or spectacular weapons of war. True power is the subversive nature of God's holy love actualized in the brokenness of the human condition—a condition that rages against the darkness with the vitality characteristic of the Holy Spirit of God. Power

---

36. 2 Cor 1:1; 8:4; 9:1, 12; 13:13. See also 13:21 for the "holy kiss."

is complete through what the cosmos deems as worthless and powerless. God's gracious favor remains the singular factor in Paul's life. As Ben Witherington notes, God's "grace was obviously strength to endure, not healing grace."[37] The manifestation of God's power in Paul's life was that God did not shield Paul from the realities of suffering; rather, God's use of Paul despite Paul's failings and agonies reminds us continually that God is at work to empower us through our sufferings, that our weaknesses are going to strengthen us with the teleological goal of union with Christ through our sufferings. We, therefore, are to strive after and persevere toward a certain teleological focal point (Rom 2:6–7), and this concept of Pauline perfectionism may be exemplified in 2 Corinthians 7:1, perhaps one the strongest texts in favor of entire sanctification:

> [Because] we have these promises, beloved ones, we should purify ourselves from all defilement of the flesh and spirit, perfecting holiness (ἐπιτελοῦντες ἁγιωσύνην) in reverence for God.[38]

Two major points must be made when discussing this text. The phrase "purify ourselves" (καθαρίσωμεν ἑαυτοὺς) suggests that this is an action undertaken by the human person. In light of the evidence above where it has been argued that Paul did not view the human person as a composite, this phrase seems to press us toward understanding Paul as saying that the human person, in response to God, has the moral responsibility and intellectual freedom to purify themselves before a holy God. Belleville notes, "in the sphere of agriculture, καθαρίζω ('to purify') means 'to prune away' or 'clear' the ground of weeds . . . both Greek religion and Judaism placed an emphasis on physical and ritual purity."[39] The active tense form of the subjunctive, when combined with the reflexive ἑαυτοὺς, makes this abundantly clear: the human person is called to cleanse herself from anything that defiles her.

The second point of sanctification centers on the participial phrase ἐπιτελοῦντες[40] ἁγιωσύνην ἐν φόβῳ θεοῦ. What does it mean to be "per-

---

37. Witherington, *Conflict and Community*, 462.

38. While some like Bultmann, *Theology*, 205, have argued that 2 Cor 6:14–7:1 is a non-Pauline interpolation, many have not found this argument to be persuasive. See Witherington, *Conflict and Community*, 402–4, who views the pericope as a "deliberate digression" rather than interpolation. The textual evidence alone suggests that the pericope is likely original despite protestations to the contrary.

39. Belleville, *2 Corinthians*, 184.

40. In Gal 3:3, Paul chides the Galatian church by asking them if they think they

fecting holiness in reverence for God"? It seems rather obvious that this phrase is centered on the work of the human person to be "perfecting" her "sanctification,"[41] something that strongly implies a free response of an assenting will. The compound verb ἐπιτελέω often refers to a "completed" action or result, and this works nicely with the reciprocal language of Philippians 1:6 where Christ is "completing" or "perfecting" a "good work" among the Philippian congregation. Christ is active in the lives of his active people, no less so in Corinth. While the triune God is certainly involved in purification elsewhere in the New Testament (see Heb 1:3 where Christ is the one "making a cleansing for sins"), Paul's language is quite clear and forceful. The human person is enjoined to seek their purification in the fear of God, and part of this process is the perfection of holiness in rejecting temple worship and cultic elements (see 2 Cor 6:14–18). Hence, Paul believed that the human person was free and able to purify himself or herself in seeking God, without respite or hesitation: sanctification is a process begun in this life, with no clarifying word to suggest that this ends upon the moment of death. Rather, the active tense form of the participle ἐπιτελοῦντες confirms the opposite: in the scheme of "already/not yet," this perfection is actualized grammatically with the notion of a completed process that will ultimately be accomplished over time. The inclusion of "flesh and spirit" (σαρκὸς καὶ πνεύματος) does not denote only the apocalyptic reality of new creation, but the transformation of current reality where flesh and spirit are rectified by God-in-Christ-by-the-Holy-Spirit in the present world, with the purpose of spreading the hope of holiness in the midst of a dying world. As John Wesley notes: flesh = outward sin; spirit = inward sin.[42] How this process looks according to 2 Corinthians 7:1 is relatively simple, and I believe Ambrosiaster is correct when he says,

> We do this [perfecting holiness] by pursuing the things which are right in the fear of God and which are therefore holy, abstaining from sins in the name of Christ. People who restrain themselves from vices without professing Christ may seem to be set apart

---

have been fuller ἐπιτελεῖσθε ("perfected"). Rather than create a problem for my thesis, it actually proves my point. Paul assumes the plausibility of perfection and insinuates that the Galatian church has not reached this potential reality because of their desire to bring back Torah.

41. Much has been written on the language of "holiness" (ἁγιωσύνην) already, but from this context it is clear that while this noun is a gift from God, a gift given in a patronage culture requires a response. See Barclay, *Paul*.

42. Wesley, *Explanatory Notes*, 460.

according to the world but not according to the Spirit of God. Only those who believe are made clean. Others, whatever they may be like, remain unclean.[43]

Similarly, the early Christian witness in interpreting this verse corresponds quite strongly to a perfectionist understanding—that is, the fear of God is a compelling (though not coercive or deterministic) method that empowers humanity to perfect themselves through the witness of the Spirit. John Chrysostom writes

> For it is possible to perfect chasteness, not in the fear of God but for vainglory. And along with this [Saint Paul] implies yet another thing, by saying, "In the fear of God;" the manner, namely, whereafter holiness may be perfected. For if lust be even an imperious thing, still if thou occupy its territory with the fear of God, thou hast stayed its frenzy.[44]

However, Ralph Martin argues against a perfectionist reading of 2 Corinthians 7:1: He writes, "Paul appears to some readers to be promoting the idea that the Corinthians are to obtain holiness by way of the observance of cultic ordinances . . . but to take this position suggests what is being advocated is instant holiness in this life. This is quite inconsistent with Paul in other places (see Phil 3:12–15)."[45]

There are a number of issues with this rebuttal. First, Paul's use of the conjunction οὖν ("therefore, since") in 7:1 presses us to consider the process of God's call: purification (*contra* defilement and idolatry) and cleansing are in response to such malignant worship practices describes in chapter 6. That is to say, Paul's response is already corrective to those who would practice such things, as Paul would later argue in 2 Timothy 2:18–22. Specifically, the reflexive ἐκκαθάρῃ ἑαυτὸν in 2 Timothy 2:21 states that this "cleansing" aspect of "sanctification" (ἡγιασμένον) is to be done by the person herself—that is, through the influence of the Spirit, but not through force. We are told to "pursue" specific Christian attributes: rectification,

---

43. *Commentary on Paul's Epistles* (CSEL 81.247).

44. Chrysostom, John. "Homilies of St. John Chrysostom, Archbishop of Constantinople, on the Second Epistle of St. Paul the Apostle to the Corinthians." In *Saint Chrysostom: Homilies on the Epistles of Paul to the Corinthians*, edited by Philip Schaff, translated by J. Ashworth and Talbot B. Chambers, 345. Vol. 12. A Select Library of the Nicene and Post-Nicene Fathers of the Christian Church, First Series. New York: Christian Literature Company, 1889. My thanks to Pastor Austin Long for this citation.

45. Martin, *2 Corinthians*, 210.

faith, love, and peace (δίωκε δὲ δικαιοσύνην, πίστιν, ἀγάπην, εἰρήνην). The abolition of our sinful passions (1 Tim 2:22) follows from the pursuit of sanctification, affirming the idea of entire sanctification as a reality into which all Christians are called to live. The human response is free, uncoerced, and divinely invited (2 Pet 1:4). To be in a state of "perfecting" holiness is to be in a place where the Holy Spirit is the chief operator in one's life: Paul assumes this pneumatic reality already in his discourses, and if the assembly is gathered, the Spirit will do mighty works.

Second, and more importantly, no one is advocating what might be called universal "instant holiness." Far from it! This is a common misunderstanding of the doctrine of entire sanctification. John Wesley notably accepted this nuance: "carrying [the perfecting aspect of holiness] to the height in all its branches, and enduring to the end in the loving fear of God, the sure foundation of all holiness."[46] Holiness may occur in an instantaneous moment, but more often than not, it is progressive and culminates later. More specifically, the active tense form of the compound participle contains the elements of actualization and continued participation in sanctification, and Martin seems to simply sidestep this issue. Third, Martin assumes that Philippians 3:12–15 and 2 Corinthians 7:1 are at odds with one another—an unnecessary interpretive move. Synergism is at play in both where both God and the human person operate together.

Thus, the language of 2 Corinthians 7:1 (and elsewhere) is decisive in summing up all that has been said so far: because the Holy Spirit is empowering the people of God, we can thus exercise our freed wills, having become a "new creation" (2 Cor 5:17), perfecting our holiness in coordination with the work of God already begun. Hence, this theological axiom covers both the anthropological dimension of the human person as formerly enslaved to sin, her need for liberation, and her continually working out of God's will and desire for her life. In a word, she is seeking the perfect things of God by the power of the perfect God.[47] The presence of sin in the life of the Christian does not logically negate the future "perfection" of her mind and heart in Christ within this lifetime. For the believer, the final removal of sin from their life remains a struggle that most often does not cease when they are called into the vocation of serving Jesus. Rather, and

---

46. Wesley, *Explanatory Notes*, 460.

47. Given the prominence in Paul's triumphal discourse in 1 Cor 15:35–57 surrounding the future resurrection of the body, one can safely see a connection between the present renewal of the human person as a somatic being and her future resurrection into pneumatic perfection.

often, it is a difficult process of seeking sanctification and holiness by the Holy Spirit; sometimes, the walk through the valley of the shadow of death is indeed filled with terrors and pain. But it is good. As Saint Basil said, "We are instructed to marvel at the unspeakable benevolence of God in Christ Jesus and with the greater fear to cleanse ourselves of every defilement of the flesh and the spirit."[48]

In Philippians, there are two specific texts that demand a close look as they pertain to the thesis of this book: 1:6 and 3:12–15. Philippians 1:6 reads as, "And I am persuaded of this, that the one who has begun a good work among you will perfect it at the day of Christ Jesus." Concerning the context, Stephen Fowl rightly suggests in relation to 1:6 that "the church is a community which has a destiny, an end, or telos given by God."[49] On the face of it, this verse suggests that God's sovereignty is active in the lives of believers (as the one working: ἐναρξάμενος) who have actively participated (v. 5: κοινωνίᾳ and v.7: συγκοινωνούς) with Paul's Gospel mission.[50] God's activity is central to the perseverance of the saints. In Philippians 1:6, we have this same compound verb (ἐπιτελέσει) where it is used to refer to the active work of Christ in the life of the Christian. Moisés Silva notes "the tension that exists between the believers' accountability for their own spiritual conduct and their need to rely totally on God's grace in order to meet that obligation."[51] While Silva correctly notes that some will resist this language as belonging to the realm of "systematic theology,"[52] I would disagree about the nature of "tension." Paul in both Epistles is focused on the mutual outworking of this process of perfection between Christians and Christ, a process where Christ and the community are both striving together toward the end. If one views Pauline perfection as a mutual process or trajectory where both the triune God and the human person, through the work of her faithful community, are striving toward the same goal, there is no tension, especially if one includes the language of being "conformed" to the image of the Son. Being conformed to the "image of God's Son" in Romans 8:29 assumes a state of (present) glorification on the part of the resurrected and

---

48. *Concerning Baptism* (FC 9:374).

49. Fowl, *Philippians*, 25.

50. This includes the missional impulse on the gospel, but also God's activity within human beings as it relates to the proclamation of the gospel.

51. Silva, *Philippians*, 45.

52. Silva, *Philippians*, 45. I personally would not object to his analysis, as I think it is coordinate with the language of Scripture and does not force a foreign category upon Paul's words.

exalted Christ, along with being "conformed to Christ's glorious body" in Philippians 3:21. In both instances, Christ's resurrection is the source of our future resurrection, glorification, and sanctification, and the present reality of transformation. This is confirmed by Paul's use of the future active verb μετασχηματίσει[53] in Philippians 3:21, and potential echoes of this language previously established in this Epistle.[54] In 3:12–15 we have something a bit different. The text reads:

> [12]*not that I have already attained this or have been perfected* (τετελείωμαι), *but I pursue it to take it for myself, upon whom even I was obtained by Christ.* [13]*Brothers and sisters, I myself do not regard this as having been obtained: but one thing I know is that I am forgetting what is behind and straining for what lies ahead.* [14]*I pursue toward the goal for the prize of the upward calling of God in Christ Jesus.* [15]*Therefore, as many of us that are perfect* (τέλειοι), *let us have this mindset,*[55] *and if you think differently about anything, God will unveil that to you also.*

Martin sees the key verb in v. 12 as referring to "knowledge."[56] Gordon Fee suggests that the verb "carries the sense of having 'been brought to completion,'"[57] which is not excluded from the realm of Christian perfection by any means. Paul's use of the perfect tense form suggests that his faith and sufferings have not yet resulted in his being perfected in Christ (3:9). The issue of separating ethics from Paul's own discourse here in Philippians suggests that Pauline interpreters are willing to overlook issues that Paul takes quite seriously. Being "perfected" by means of suffering (3:11) means that Paul desires to be united to Christ through suffering (3:10): the death of Christ is the ocean that we are to dive into if we are to follow him (John 21:18–19). To remove ethics and the moral demands of being in Christ from this entire discussion is unnecessary:

---

53. The symmetry or reciprocity of μετασχηματίσει and Christ's subjection of all things work together and needn't be set in opposition to the other if one assumes a mutual outworking of these concepts.

54. Fee notes that these verbs "pick up the language of [Phil 2:6-8], where Christ, who was in the 'form' (*morphē*) of God, assumed the 'form' of a slave in coming in the 'likeness' (*schēma*) of human beings." See Fee, *Paul's Letter*, 382. More likely, however, is Paul's closer thematic use of συμμορφιζόμενος τῷ θανάτῳ αὐτοῦ ("Being conformed/formed with his death") in Phil 3:10. The language assumes mutual participatory suffering on the part of the Philippian church, and does not exclude a mutual participation of imitation of Christ.

55. Flemming, *Philippians*, 192, offers this translation.

56. Martin, *Philippians*, 206.

57. Fee, *Paul's Letter*, 344.

THE PERFECTION OF OUR FAITHFUL WILLS

do we really believe Paul's ethical standards were cast aside in this discussion? Paul's sense of the language is clear: he has not yet attained "perfection," and the interplay between Christ claiming Paul and Paul claiming Christ[58] suggests synergism. Paul is not a passive object within God's story; rather Paul is an active agent at play in God's mission, seeking the final goal and pressing toward it, with the apocalyptic hope that he would attain it (3:11).

The lack of this "perfection" in 3:12 does not suggest that Paul did not believe in being "perfected" by the Spirit. Rather, Paul never mitigates or downplays the threat of passivity and apathy. The journey of faith is a journey toward the telic Christ by the power of the Spirit, where union with Christ is enfleshed and where all fear is cast asunder. As Flemming has noted, the adjective τέλειοι ("perfect") in 3:15 when used in the LXX "can describe those whose hearts are wholly devoted to God (2 Kings 8:61; 11:4; 15:3; 20:3)."[59] While this meaning is certainly to be included within the realm of possibility, another element should be considered—that element being having the "mindset of Christ" (2:4–5), which includes ambition toward ethical praxis and the person being entirely united to Christ. Sanctification, glorification, and the empowerment of the Spirit are hence integrated together at this point, as we are conformed into Christ and his faithfulness. The temporal reality of sin and the struggle against evil does not mitigate the call toward entire sanctification; rather, the call is intensified as we respond through the work of the Holy Spirit against sin with the goal to be united fully to Christ in holy love. The intense struggle of sanctification is a progression into the apocalyptic unknown, where the Spirit of God is active and moving despite any restrictions we may place upon the Spirit.

Moving on to Paul's Epistle to the Colossians, we immediately see something a bit different from the material we saw in Philippians. Christology of course plays a large part in the structure of Philippians, but the exegesis of certain sections of Colossians (1:28; 3:14; 4:12) must be centered on perseverance and sanctification in a way that Philippians does not. Christ is the one who is both Creator and sustainer of the cosmos (1:15–20), the one who has reconciled all things to God (1:20–22) and has called the church toward faithful persistence in Christ (1:23). These people were "at one time hostile" (ποτε: 1:21), but in God's new apocalyptic schema have been reconciled and rectified in Christ (Rom 3:21–26). This is a present and

58. Flemming, *Philippians*, 184.
59. Flemming, *Philippians*, 193.

established new order under the kingship of Christ; gone are the hostility and evil deeds done in the past. The new humanity has been established in Christ and through Christ.

Colossians 1:28 begins with an admonition toward all believers:

> Him we proclaim, warning all people and teaching all people in all wisdom, so that we might present all people as perfect (τέλειον) in Christ.

The ESV renders τέλειον as "mature," but this is imprecise and theologically insufficient for Paul's purpose here.[60] Fundamental to Paul's claim is the invasive presence of Christ in the entire cosmic world and realm, including being operative with humanity and the church as their "head." Christ's headship (κεφαλή) throughout Colossians (1:18; 2:10, 19) is rather explicit: Christ is the "head" or "provision" of the body (1:18); head and body are interdependent upon one another and cannot be separated. While "head" (κεφαλή) can refer to "preeminence,"[61] the explicit focus in Colossians is on Christ as the Creator.[62] Christ is also the "origin" of the various "sovereignties" (2:10) that were explicitly created by God-in-Christ in Colossians 1:16. More specifically, the somatic nature of the Christ-church relation is exemplified in 2:19 where the human person must cling to the "head" (κεφαλήν), which is the fountainhead of our "growth" (αὔξει). Christ's headship, then, is not about Christ being portrayed as an authority, but rather as the sustainer of the life of his church. Thus, for Colossians 1:28, we see that the "perfection" of the human person is located within the "sphere" (ἐν) of Christ by means of reconciliation and union with him. This is our apocalyptic "hope of glory" (δόξης; 1:27) where humanity struggles along with the active and risen Christ (1:29) in order to be united fully and perfectly to him. The telic ideal and reality of Christ's reign involves our "bearing good fruit" and "growing" in the knowledge of Christ (Col 1:10), which is an explicitly ethical category. Similarly, Colossians 3:14 says that "love" is the "bond that binds everything together in perfection (τελειότητος)." This

---

60. The use of ἵνα ("so that") suggests a purpose clause, where the result of "admonishing/teaching" in all "wisdom" is that people would be "perfect" in Christ." See Harris, *Colossians & Philemon*, 73.

61. Eph 1:22.

62. Westfall, *Paul and Gender*, 80–84; Thiselton, *First Epistle*, 812–22 for the various nuances. I, for one, think there one can interpret κεφαλή as meaning "preeminent" in certain contexts (LXX) but "source" as a metaphor makes good sense of several of Paul's uses of the word.

contains a serious ethical admonition toward all people, especially as this "bond of perfection" is previously defined as "compassion, kindness," and so forth (3:12–13). This includes the "forgiveness of sins" (1:14), an assertion that is tied up with Christ's apocalyptic emancipatory act of liberation. Hence, Colossians 1:28 makes good sense in supporting the doctrine of Christian perfection, especially when related to the "already/not yet" aspect of salvation within Colossians.[63] Paul's ethics are wrapped up in the goal of transforming people into being "perfect" in Christ, and by Christ's vocational power and desire to reconcile all things together. Sin is to be abolished by the Christocentric life. As Marianne Meye Thompson has eloquently said, "'perfect in Christ' implies transformation into the likeness of Christ, who is the image of God (1:15)."[64] However, Scot McKnight argues that τέλειον "does not point toward a rigid sense of sinlessness. Rather [the term] combines conformity to the moral purity of God as taught by Jesus and the apostles (Matt 5:48)."[65] In response, it must be noted that these two ideas (sinlessness vs. moral purity) are clearly not at odds with each other.[66] In Paul's discourses on perfection he often explicitly talks about ethics and sin (2 Cor 7:1) and clearly says that sin will have its final and irrevocable end eventually—but it is not at all certain that one's sinful desires are terminated at the resurrection. Rather, Paul seems to strongly suggest the opposite. The nature of sanctification is the destruction of the "body of sin" (metaphorically speaking) and the embrace of the holy life. This is summed up under Paul's theology of reconciliation (Col 1:19–20) as the corrupt powers are stripped of their privilege and sovereignty (2:14). Therefore, the notion of being confirmed to the sinlessness of Christ's own resurrected reality informs us of our calling and God's desire: for us to be fully like Christ, and this includes the destruction of the body of sin.

One of Paul's final parting words in Colossians that is related to our discussion can be found in 4:12:

> *Epaphras, who is one of you, a slave of Christ, greets you. He is struggling always for you in prayer, so that you might stand perfect and*

---

63. In some sense also, if one wanted to be rather cheeky one might argue that Christian perfection is an element that might make the case for the Pauline authorship of Colossians.

64. Thompson, *Colossians & Philemon*, 46.

65. McKnight, *Epistle to Colossians*, 202–3.

66. One also might sense an implicit critique of legalism in McKnight's comments here. This is a concern I share and one that I will attempt to respond to below.

fully fulfilled (τέλειοι καὶ πεπληροφορημένοι) *in the entire will of God.*

Similar to Colossians 1:28 is the "so that" (ἵνα) clause, with the goal of the human person standing firm[67] or strong in perfection and comprehensive or complete "fulfillment."[68] The relationship between "perfect" and "fully fulfilled" suggests a theological correspondence: being described as both perfect and fully fulfilled is included within God's will, for the purpose of glorification. The completeness of a person in Christ means the full measure of holiness has overflowed in their life. The language of "fulfillment" throughout Colossians refers to human fulfillment in knowledge (Col 1:9; 2:10), the God-Christ relationship (1:19), and Christ's own bodily incarnation of deity (2:9).[69] Here, God's will is acting with Epaphras' prayers for those in Colossae for their perfection despite the various opponents. The hope of glory for us is that God would entirely sanctify us from our sins and that God might beckon us into perfect union with him. The presentation of humanity before God as "perfect and fully fulfilled" suggests that this reality is not confined to the eschaton but is to be made manifest now. Christ's presence and work are not limited to the end of all things; rather, God is active through God's word, for us and for our salvation. Epaphras' own struggle is magnified in our struggle as the people of God, to present our lives to God—not because of our works but because of our vocation in serving the God of the universe. Those who are in Christ are already participating in what God has called them to and their sanctification is set in motion: "perfect, endued with every Christian grace."[70] The penultimate goal of God's work in Christ is to liberate us from sin and bondage to decay; sanctification thus becomes an enabling agent through prevenient grace[71]

---

67. Paul's use of the aorist transitive verb "might stand" (σταθῆτε) means that there is no direct object for the verb.

68. The goal of sanctification and "standing firm" (στηρίξαι) in 1 Thess 3:13 means that the person is "blameless in holiness," where purification has resulted in the person being set free from the power and sphere of sin.

69. This verse is not merely describing the representation of "Deity/divinity" (τῆς θεότητος), as in Jesus was representing deity by being human. It is an assertion of Christ's own preexistence described in Col 1:14–20 and given full force in 2:9, where the humanness of Christ and the divinity of Christ are seen as complementary images that paint a holistic Christological portrait.

70. Wesley, *Explanatory Notes*, 524.

71. For a biblical and theological case for prevenient grace, see Shelton, *Prevenient Grace*.

THE PERFECTION OF OUR FAITHFUL WILLS

to empower people to live the life God has gifted to them. In Paul's concluding benediction (*peroratio*) to the Thessalonian assembly (1 Thess 5:23), we have these words written for us:

> And may he, the God of peace, sanctify you entirely (ἁγιάσαι . . . ὁλοτελεῖς) and may your whole[72] (ὁλόκληρον) spirit and person[73] and body be preserved as blameless in the coming of our Lord Jesus Christ.

Several things must be noted within this short verse. First, God is the agent here, but God is not to be separated from the work of Jesus. Both are involved in the apocalyptic reality of deliverance from sin. Second, the hapax legomena adjective ὁλοτελεῖς is a compound of ὅλος ("whole, all") and τέλος ("goal, end"). BDAG 4559 defines the compound as "'meeting a high standard of perfection', perfect in every way." The importance of this verse is that it comes directly after Paul's explicit call to "keep away from every form of evil" (1 Thess 5:22)—hence the whole issue of entire sanctification centers on the rejection of sin (1 Thess 2:10). Paul's use of the verb ἁγιάσαι reflects the LXX use of the term: the sanctification of a holy mountain or a place of sacred architecture (Exod 19:23; 2 Chr 2:3), an animal sacrifice (Exod 29:1, 33, 36) and even with respect to God (Num 20:12; 27:14). First Esdras 1:3 speaks of temple servants "sanctifying themselves" (ἁγιάσαι) before God as well, which is similar to 1 Thess 5:23, although Paul's Epistle lacks the overt cultic connotations.

We are to be "without blame" (ἀμέμπτως) in what God has called us to be: a people set apart and dedicated solely to God. This verse explicitly affirms God's work—not merely the human process—in our sanctification, and the entirety of the sanctifying process is not to be pressed entirely into the future. Rather, the aorist tense form suggests that this is a process that has already begun and will continue,[74] and I see no reason why this sanctifying process will terminate only and exclusively within the eschatological new creation. The present call is a call for all people to participate *now* in what God has done and what God is doing. The apocalyptic reality of God's

---

72. "The word signifies wholly and perfectly; every part and all that concerns you; all that is of, or about you." Wesley, *Explanatory Notes*, 532.

73. As we saw above, Paul's use of "soul" (ἡ ψυχὴ) more likely corresponds to the idea of "person" or "vitality" as opposed to the idea of an immortal immaterial soul.

74. "This text suggests they are involved in the process of sanctification by virtue of what they do or do not do. For this reason we must interpret the aorist opative ἁγιάσαι as embracing the whole process," Wanamaker, *Epistles*, 206.

invasive work for fallen humanity is a conclusive demonstration of God's kindness in Christ: sanctification is the catalyst for the life of holiness and the Holy Spirit is the agent who presses us into full unity with the triune God and with one another.

3.3: Baptism & Perfection

A major theme that is vital to the doctrine of entire sanctification is the sacrament of baptism. The Gospel of Matthew speaks of "baptism" leading to the "confessing of sins" (Matt 3:6). Related to baptism act is the need for the confession of sins and the life of holy love: the outpouring of the Holy Spirit (Matt 3:11). The Spirit and Jesus Christ are distinct but not inseparable as the means of baptism in the life of the believer. Baptism "into Christ" is a baptism into his life and death (Rom 6:3–4; Gal 3:27; Col 2:12), and the Spirit is the source of our spiritual vitality and giftedness (1 Cor 12:13). Baptism is the well from which the doctrine of entire sanctification drinks. Perhaps the most succinct statement is the creedal formulation in Ephesians 4:5: "one Lord, one Spirit, one baptism." When the one who professes allegiance to Christ operates by faith in what God is doing in their life (Col 2:12), sanctification begins: as we are immersed into Christ's death, we are raised by the power of God. Baptism is the means by which a person is pressed into the depths of death and given new life in the Spirit as she is drawn and clothed in Christ. Baptism leads to the death of the self to sin and the emergence of new life. Thus, the road of sanctification has begun through immersion and emergence into the new life of the Spirit.

3:4: Conclusion: Paul's Apocalyptic Vision of Perfection

> For many years I have preached, 'there is a love of God that casts out all sin.' Convince me that this word has fallen to the ground, that in twenty years none has attained this love, that there is no living witness of it at this day, and I will preach it no more.
> —John Wesley[75]

Here we see the threads from above (Christology and anthropology) come together. Christ as the perfect one, the preexistent and eternal Son, is the one who leaped into the realm of the forsaken and the enslaved. The imperfect,

---

75. Outler, *John Wesley*, 298.

the wretched, the incarcerated are reckoned as righteous and rectified by his work. The material world order, with our bodies, is seen for what it is: enslavement and disempowerment and dehumanization. The notion of the immortality of the human soul is a prerogative that must be questioned, but not dismissed outright due to its pride of place within the Christian tradition.[76] The immortal God became mortal for us, and those who are mortal will be made immortal by his power in the end. The distinction between the immortal God and mortal humanity is a necessary distinction that must be made in order not to collapse eschatology entirely into the present. Entire sanctification is apocalyptic; the resurrection unto immortality and glory is eschatological. Immortality is a gift contained within the very nature of God and this gift is only granted in the eschatological sense to those who have participated in God's vocation of holy love and allegiance. Hence, the reason we ought to conceive of Paul's anthropology in material terms is to maintain the distinction between the Creator and the created order. Creation is marred by catastrophe and violence, whereas God is sinless and without blemish, and this distinction must be made as we continue on in our exploration of the doctrine of entire sanctification. The call into unity with Christ calls us to envision the power of God through the Holy Spirit as being that which attests to our transformation.

As we have seen above, several key texts seem to directly assert that "perfection" in terms of sanctification is attainable in this life (2 Cor 7:1), and other texts strongly imply it (Col 1:28; 4:12; Phil 3:12–15; Rom 12:2; 15:16). It also seems that large parts of Paul's theology, particularly his eschatology and ethical stances, presuppose the perfective work of the Spirit; Paul's robust pneumatology presses directly against the notion that the Spirit is incapable of empowering people toward perfection before their death. The doctrine of Christian perfection also lies behind all of Paul's ethical injunctions to his various assemblies: the abandonment of sin is the ultimate goal, to present people as being liberated entirely from the power of sin and finally death (1 Cor 15:24–26). The biblical theme of emancipation from sin and enslavement is woven in the narrative of Scripture, and the consequence of entire sanctification—for the purpose of empowering others to live into Christ—is a likely pneumatic reality.

For all Christians, the ultimate goal is to be united entirely to Christ without hesitation or partiality. Within the sphere of the human agent operating in the sphere of God's calling and prevenient grace, the hope of

---

76. See 5.3 below.

glory is exercising persuasion upon people, beckoning them to God-in-Christ. Empowered by the Holy Spirit, the person is freed to respond to God's initiating call upon them, and the people who yield and freely unite themselves to God will be sanctified. The call of holiness is not merely the journey through the dark valley of the soul; rather, the call to holiness is not to be reserved for one's self. For those who are struggling with what God has called them to be, there is hope. Christ's own life—modeled in his healings, his kindness, his subversive grace, and his sacrificial death—is our life to live in faithful allegiance. The Christian life is a call to holiness, unreserved in our love for God and neighbor, cooperating with the Spirit to be the people whom God desires us to be. We are to reject the vision the world asserts as providing moral and spiritual satisfaction. Rather, our satisfaction is to be grounded in Christ through the Spirit, and this means a life lived in active rebellion against sin and all that entails the life of the world. Entire sanctification, for Paul, is an apocalyptic assault against the worldliness and licentiousness and oppressiveness that encapsulated the Roman Empire and the empires of today. Holiness is God's weapon to wield against what enslaves humanity, and Paul's call to holiness is a call to arms.

The next two chapters of this work will focus on two test cases: specifically, the question of sex and marriage and the question about eschatology, and how entire sanctification impacts both issues in light of what we have seen above. For those who are in Christ and living by the Spirit, we will see how marriage and the future break into our present reality.

4

Sex & Sanctification in Pauline Perspective

4.1: Holy Sex: Introduction

Scripture's rather diverse perspective on sex and gender has provoked no small measure of conflict and speculation. For women involved in ordained ministry, this question has no doubt been a source of great pain in their lives, especially as it relates to how people are treated. The goal of this chapter is to tease out Paul's logic on perfection and apply it to sexuality and gender in his Epistles. For many, these texts are familiar and well traversed. Almost every book on Paul and "gender roles" explicitly utilizes these texts, sometimes to narrow effect; my goal is not to argue for a full-fledged view of women in ministry and marriage[1] but to illustrate Christian perfection as Paul does in his texts on marriage.

4.1a: Singleness & Sanctification

Most often in this discussion, a book would turn directly to marriage as being that which most completely reveals Jesus to us: the one who is united to his bride (Eph 5:25). However, one must pause before entering such a

---

1. The honor of that work in my opinion belongs to Cynthia Westfall's, *Paul and Gender*.

discussion. For Paul and Paul's mission, the goal is singleness (1 Cor 7:7–9), and he himself was single.[2] This was a pragmatic move, I suspect on his part. So any discussion must begin with what Paul desired (singleness) before we place marriage upon a holy pedestal at the expense of our single brothers and sisters. Sanctification for the single person is not to be found uniformly in marriage; the calling of holiness is greater than the call to marriage, and the church should give great pause before worshiping marriage at the expense of single people in our midst.[3] Singleness is not a deformity; singleness is not a character flaw or defect; singleness is not something that must always be rectified.[4] Singleness is an appropriate and godly vocation that many denigrate and few are willing to explore—although this appears to be changing for the better.[5] One must never forget that the eternal Son of God never sought marriage, never sought sex, and lived a life of complete celibacy. We have numerous men and women throughout Scripture who exercised leadership in various communities—such as the women who funded Jesus' ministry (Luke 8:1-3) and the women and men of Rom 16—whose vocation was not shattered or demeaned by their singleness. Far from it! There is a stronger case for singleness in the Christian life than there is for marriage.[6] In the Christian church—especially the evangelical wing that I am a part of—marriage is exalted as the primary (only?) means of sanctification and satisfaction in this life. This is something I believe has done great harm to the church.

4.2: She Makes Him Holy: Perfection & Mutuality in Marriage

In the evangelical "gender debate," Ephesians 5:21–33 is at the center of almost every discussion on marriage in the Bible. This is unfortunate, as

---

2. One might also note that our Lord and Savior—the perfect one—was also single.

3. For a sobering and powerful work that explores this question, see Hill, *Spiritual Friendship*.

4. I have numerous friends who have struggled as single men and women in trying to find work in the church, and this is something the church must rectify. Being single in the church is often the greatest barrier to vocational service, and this should give the church great pause before drawing up unbiblical restrictions that bar women and men from service and leadership.

5. John Stott, who had a major influence on my own theological journey, was single his entire life. See Stott and Hsu, "John Stott."

6. Hitchcock, *Significance of Singleness*.

that text is not at all the longest text on marriage nor is it the text that is the most practical and inclusive. That honor belongs to 1 Corinthians 7:1–16, and this text deserves specific attention first, especially as a hermeneutical lens by which we can understand everything else Paul has written. In this large chapter, several aspects of our discussion lie at the center of Paul's text. Paul begins with a response to the Corinthians' question (7:1), and his response is a concession based upon sexual temptation (πορνείας) in 7:2. However, Paul's vision of mutuality immediately surfaces when he speaks about each spouse in exactly parallel ways in 7:2,

> "Each man should have (ἐχέτω) his own wife and each woman should have (ἐχέτω) her own husband."

The marital union of the wife and the husband centers on mutual possession, where the imperatival nature of Paul's language presses against the sexual dysfunction found in 1 Corinthians 5:1. Here, mutuality is already present and assumed in Paul's logic. Both spouses mutually possess one another with equal authority and insight and power. Both have their "own" (ἴδιον) spouse, where Paul is clearly identifying personal agency on their behalf. Each spouse is "owed a marital duty" (ὀφειλὴν), which probably includes sex but is likely more than just that (7:3)—sex is never simply about sex. This outlook on marital sex is incredibly progressive, as Paul is affirming that a husband owes his wife something in the same way that she owes him, and that both have urges, desires, giftings, and needs.[7] Ron Pierce suggests, "In this case, the husband—the one with greater power and status—is called upon first to yield by giving what rightfully belongs to his wife. Then, to be complete, the wife is told the same obligation applies to her."[8] Authority is something exercised mutually in 7:4, where neither spouse can claim preeminence over the other, especially at the expense of the other. A husband and a wife explicitly have authority in this relationship (ἐξουσιάζει), which is the most explicit language of "leadership/authority/sovereignty" we have in the New Testament as it relates to so-called "authority" in marriage. In 7:5 Paul orders the wife and the husband together: "do not deprive one another" (μὴ ἀποστερεῖτε ἀλλήλους). As the husband has certain physical needs, so does the wife; neither spouse is to be used in this relationship solely for the purpose of pleasure. Paul's counter-cultural

---

7. The adverb ὁμοίως ("likewise") proves this point, that both people have an equal requirement to grant sexual pleasure to the other.

8. Pierce, "First Corinthians," 8.

sexual ethic here is on full display. A wife is not to be subordinated to the needs and desires of her husband; rather, the husband is to consider the needs and desires of his wife before his own, and the wife is to do likewise. This text establishes the equality of husband and wife in marriage and the mutuality of sex between them affirms the spousal needs of the other and calls them holy and good before God. Mutuality is God's design for marriage, not patriarchy or matriarchy. To put a finer point on it, Paul asserts that a woman's sexual needs are not to be viewed through the lens of male desires, but the opposite: both husband and wife are to understand and respect the desires of the other, seeking to build one another up and not reduce them to a sexual subordinate. As such, sinful entities like pornography are a stifling and lasting evil that infects both men and women with the belief that their desires are to be seen in opposition or competition to their spouse. Sex, in Paul's perspective, is the opposite of this worldly facade: sexual desire is found in the dignity and humanity of your spouse, not in disjointed preferences and selfishness.

Paul sees a wife, contrary to many elements of the ancient world, as someone with God-given sexual agency and God-given sexual desires—and this is a good thing according to Paul! When one hears sex talked about from the pulpit, should you be so lucky, it is almost always talked about from a male perspective, where the wife's sole mission is to placate or satisfy the urges of her husband.[9] This runs in direct contradiction to Paul's admonition toward mutual submission. Instead of applying male privilege or dominance to the conversation, Paul vociferously condemns this selfish mindset by strongly asserting the holiness of a wife's sexual agency and needs without shame or contempt for a woman's body or mind. Both are sexual creatures, different by design, clothed in the dignity of Christ. Hence, any "deprivation" from either spouse must be done "mutually" or by "mutual consent" (συμφώνου). The sexual desires and interests of the wife are protected, affirmed, and taken into account as the marriage relationship operates. Neither is given sexual preeminence, and both are to affirm the goodness and holiness of the other's body. To participate in sexual hierarchalism is an affront to holiness and Christlikeness. Paul's concession to the couple is in favor of his desire for singleness (7:6–9). Paul states that both husband and wife are not to divorce each other (7:10–11).[10] To those who

---

9. One is invited to recall the rather infamous legacy of Mark Driscoll here, should you desire to do so.

10. Richard Hays notes that Paul is explicitly appealing to the Jesus tradition here,

are in a mixed marriage (theologically speaking) Paul suggests that both husband and wife have the right to divorce one another, continuing his intentional mutual symmetry between both partners. For our purposes in this chapter, what Paul says explicitly in 7:14–16 is the heart of this passage.

> ¹⁴For the unbelieving husband is made holy (ἡγίασται) by the wife, and the unbelieving wife is made holy (ἡγίασται) by the husband: otherwise your children would be unclean, but now they are holy (ἅγιά). ¹⁵But if the faithless one separates, let them separate: a brother or sister is not enslaved by such things. God has called you to peace. ¹⁶For what do you know, wife, whether you will save (σώσεις) your husband? Or what do you know, husband, whether you will save (σώσεις) your wife?[11]

Yet again, Paul's symmetrical mutualism reigns over his advice here. Sanctification in this mixed-marriage context includes the salvific intent of the believing spouse for the other. Even the children are seen as being under the authority of both parents by use of the plural pronoun (ὑμῶν). Sex and sanctification are intertwined here, and neither spouse is permitted to dominate or seek their own sexual gratification. Salvation in this context comes by means of the faithful spouse (male or female), and to suggest that male headship is the governing prism by which we are to understand marriage is to undermine the basic thrust of Paul's language here. Nowhere does authority come into the picture except by means of mutual reciprocity and sexual necessity. Cynthia Westfall makes this powerful point:

> Paul's letters are remarkably free from Greek cultural ideas drawn from Aristotle and others about the essential differences between men and women as demonstrated in the sex act.[12] He contradicts the Greco-Roman belief that the man shows dominance through penetration and the wife is submissive through being penetrated; in Paul's model, both exercise authority and have power while they are equally mastered by the other, as in Song of Songs.[13]

---

and the impact of this shows the close relationship between Paul and that tradition. *First Corinthians*, 120.

11. This "salvation" is clearly eschatological in nature, but eschatology cannot be punted into the eschaton. Rather, salvation is an unfolding present process that begins with transformation now.

12. Althought it is crudely stated, Paul strongly denies men the 'right' of "fornication" in 1 Thess 4:3–5.

13. Westfall, *Paul and Gender*, 196.

Therefore, whenever one comes to a favorite prooftext concerning marriage (Eph 5:22), one must consider what Paul has said elsewhere explicitly about what the marriage relationship is to be governed by: mutuality, deference, respect, kindness, and genuine reciprocity. To limit 1 Corinthians 7:1–16 exclusively to sexual relationships misses the rather basic notion that sex is never simply about sex. Sex as a physiological and spiritual act is far more than a mere biological function; to suggest otherwise is to degrade and demean what God has gifted to us as embodied creatures. When it comes to the doctrine of entire sanctification, marriage can be a means by which a person grows in their journey toward becoming whom God has called them to be. Sexual intimacy in a marital relationship can be a form of sanctification, although sanctification is not to be reduced to this specific mechanism. Sex, when properly acted upon, can be an element of what God uses to sanctify a person, to make them holy by means of the spiritual authority of the other spouse. This suggests that human freedom in participating in God's vocation of holiness requires significant effort in discipling others in the ways of grace and holiness. Jesus' central point in Mark 10:1–12 (Matt 19:1ff par) is that if a husband or a wife divorces unjustly, he or she is sinning against their former spouse: a radically egalitarian notion that shows continuity between Paul and Jesus as it regards sexual ethics. Where the Pharisees present the man as the one initiating divorce (Matt 19:3), Jesus takes them back to God's ideal in Genesis 1:26–28 and places the burden of sin upon the husband who unjustly divorces his wife. Hence, marriage is a symbolic act where equality and desire are woven together as a means toward holiness. The human will, when called by God, becomes active in response to what God desires through desire for one another. The beauty of self-sacrifice and placing our desires within the intimacy of marriage plays into how Paul will later describe Christ's relationship with the church in Ephesians 5:21–33. It remains to be said that both husbands and wives have a specific calling to seek one another in mutual sanctification by the Spirit, and the idea of a gendered hierarchy is notoriously absent from Paul's language here.[14] Husbands and wives are equal participants in each other's sanctification. Feminist Katherine Bushnell's stinging remark rings clear over this text:

---

14. Paul takes great pains in his syntax to include women and men together on equal terms and with equal footing. I have not been able to find a comparable instance in the ancient world where an author comes close to being as egalitarian as Paul.

> The Apostle Paul . . . makes the authority of the wife precisely equal to the husbands in the marriage relation . . . We are quite aware that this verse [v. 4] has been reduced to a mere sophism by Bible commentaries. But "authority" does not mean "authority" at all, unless it comprehends the idea of being able to act with perfect independence either one was or in the precisely opposite way.[15]

Additional elements of marital sanctification include Paul's words in Ephesians 5:25–30:

> [25]Husbands, love your wives, just as also Christ loved the assembly and handed himself over for her sake [26]so that he might sanctify her, cleansing her with the washing[16] of water by the word, [27]so that he might present it [the church] to himself as honorable,[17] without blemish or wrinkle or anything like that so that it [the church] might be holy and blameless. [28]In this same way, husbands are obligated to love their wives as their own bodies: whoever loves his wife loves himself. [29]For no one has ever hated their own flesh, but nourishes and comforts it, just as also Christ does for the assembly. [30]For we are members of his body.

Several points must be addressed before we continue the conversation. The first major point is that joint reciprocity is a governing syntactical mandate between husband and wife (5:21): "submitting to one another in reverence for Christ." The lack of a verb for "submission" in 5:22[18] suggests that whatever submission means in this context (v. 22f), it must also be concerned with reciprocity and mutuality,[19] not on some vague notion of modernistic male headship. This is especially clear if we take 1 Corinthians 7:1-16 into account when discussing this so-called "subordinationist" text. The wife's submission (vv. 23–24) is given a general overview without

---

15. Bushnell, *God's Word*, 111.

16. Lit., "the act of bathing, washing" (τῷ λουτρῷ). LS 26719 suggests that this word refers to "a bath, a bathing place." This will be important below.

17. This word (ἔνδοξον) refers to an "honored" member of society (Luke 7:25), a speech by Jesus (Luke 13:17), and those who are "honorable" in Christ (1 Cor 4:10). Hence, Paul is probably thinking about the honored nature of the church, as the husband's treatment of his wife makes her an honored partner, not merely someone who is splendid or pleasing to his senses.

18. Our earliest manuscripts P46 and Codex Vaticanus do not have the verb for submit in v. 22.

19. The principle of "headship" in vv. 23-24 is clarified as a somatic relationship where both husband and wife are united as one flesh (5:31; Gen 2:20-24); it has nothing to do authority.

much particularity—"wifely" submission was a given in the ancient world, so Paul does not see fit to address what this would look like. The audience knows so there is no need to explain or clarify.[20]

However, the submission on the part of the husband, as we've seen, is an entirely different enterprise. Husbandly submission was not a given, nor was there a clear example where the husband yielded himself to his wife. Paul has to explain what this looks like. In a Christian context, the husband must learn how to lovingly yield to his wife and what this looks like, as opposed to unchecked masculine authoritarianism. A husband is to "love" (ἀγαπᾶτε) his wife to the point of death, and not to place her in a position where she is marginalized, abused, exploited, or burdened—especially by him. Because all people within the assembly are to be imitators of God (Eph 5:1-2), submission and love are not exclusively male traits. Rather, imitation of God is a decidedly *Christian* trait where both husband and wife are united in spirit and heart. A wife's love for her husband is not excluded by this passage; instead the husband, who had complete freedom in the ancient world to seek any sort of sexual proclivity he desired with whomever he wanted, has that privilege taken away.[21] Christ, as the example[22] given for the husband, makes the church holy (ἁγιάσῃ) by performing rather tedious activities in the ancient household; in essence, the husband submits to his wife by not treating her as a doormat and by participating with her in holiness.[23] How a husband submits is that he serves his wife: "cleansing her,"[24] "treating her with honor," and specifically fulfilling his obligations to her (1 Cor 7:3-5). We must ask, "what does a husband's submission to his wife look like in an ancient culture where men had all of the power?" As such, Paul's command for the husband to "love" his wife and to humble himself in service to her needs is Paul's way of describing submission. The

---

20. Cohick, *Women in World*.

21. Early Christianity was distinct in demanding fidelity and loyalty from *both* the wife and the husband—especially the husband. Hurtado, *Destroyer*, 166.

22. What is fascinating about this entire discussion is that many are willing to assert that examples are gender-exclusive things, where the example of Christ is totalizing, being only and forever applicable to men. This is not how Christians determine virtue or character at all, and this removes the heart of biblical ethics entirely from Scripture and our call to live our lives in holiness. An example given is not only for one person, as if a wife is not allowed to love her husband.

23. Westfall, *Paul and Gender*, 92.

24. This is not an exclusively male prerogative, as the entire church is told to "purify themselves" in 2 Cor 7:1.

husband is even told to "nourish" and "comfort" his wife (5:29)! Rather than being emasculating, Paul's language shows the powerful expectations placed upon a husband who desires to be faithful to Christ: he is to submit to his wife by treating her as his equal, respecting her, gifting her with honor, treating her as he would want to be treated, and displaying God's reckless holy love toward her. At the heart of Christian marriage is the emphasis on deference in love. How a husband would like to be treated is exactly shown by how he should treat his wife (5:28).[25] Instead of being concerned about hierarchy or male-female preferences and "roles," Paul has offered us a unique vision of marriage where both partners mutually make each other holy by participation in the things of the Spirit—marriage being a prime but not exclusive example. This aspect or method of sanctification can take many forms: an act of grace in serving someone after a difficult day of work, listening to your spouse when they are struggling, being a rock of safety for them, and allowing yourself to be vulnerable when needed. One can also be active in showing tenderness and charity instead of scorn or condescension to their spouse. The grace of empowering one another to be free from sinful desires and selfish longings is the very mark of the Spirit in our lives, and a husband and a wife are called to exercise that spiritual insight toward each other. Paul's central point is that a husband or a wife is not to be passive and removed from the spiritual life of the other—far from it. In a world where sex is treated as something cheap, Paul reminds us that one's spouse is where one can find fulfillment and pleasure and personal enrichment, not conquest and pity or domination. Both husband and wife are capable of virtue, godly character, and exercising influence to loving form one another toward union with Christ and with one another. When both husband and wife are united in this goal, then entire sanctification is unavoidable.

4.3: Gender & Vocation:
The Church as an Agent of Sanctification

For all of the power within the text, Ephesians 5:21–33 is not exclusively about the doctrine of the church. The texts above (especially 1 Cor 7) do

---

25. More specifically, the subject of the metaphor becomes unique: if the husband is the head and husband and wife are one flesh, then his wife must be his body (Eph 5:28), Note that the wife has now becomes the male in the metaphor." Westfall, *Paul and Gender*, 94.

not tell us entirely about how the church is to be run, or how the church can be a place for discipleship. However, the closest texts we have from Paul that explain his view of the church are related to his doctrine of the Spirit; specifically, Paul's eschatology is fundamentally pneumatic, where the Spirit is sovereign in the gifting of leadership and preaching the word, where "faithful people" (2 Tim 2:2) teach others.[26] The goal of the church in being united to Christ is to empower women and men to serve and participate in what God is doing. No gift is granted solely for the pleasure of one person: a gift must be shared. The gift of joy must be used for the benefit and empowerment of others. Even in our greatest tragedies, there may be a time when one's pain might be a blessing to another.

Where the Spirit is, there is ecclesiology.

4.3a: The Gifts of the Spirit: Vocation, Baptism, & Sanctification

Paul's largest and most influential discourse on the Spirit and ecclesiological gifts can be found in 1 Corinthians 12–14, where he directly says that all of the gifts given (12:4) are for the "common good" (συμφέρον: 12:7b). God's empowering work in the church is never for the narcissist or polemicist; it is not an exclusive gift that is designed to benefit only one person. Consider this: a man comes clean about his drug addiction, and in a miraculous act of grace the Spirit removes that addiction. His wife is now blessed with a husband who is consumed by what the Spirit is doing, and their children are involved as well. Holiness and the work of the Spirit are contagious, especially as they relate to the church and our witness. The "differences" (διαίρεσις: 12:4–6) of the spiritual gifts indicate genuine diversity among the people of Corinth as to their calling and gifting. The triune God[27] is the one to grants these gifts to God's people as the Spirit wills (12:11). The edification of the body is at play here in 1 Corinthians 12–14 and the de-hierarchization of the church is predicated upon the unity and diversity of the body of Christ: "For just as the body is one and has many members, and all of the members of the body, being many, are one body, so it is with Christ" (1 Cor 12:12).[28] Baptism, as the punctiliar

---

26. The Greek text reads πιστοῖς ἀνθρώποις, which is gender-inclusive. Any English translation that renders the phrase as "faithful men" is misleading.

27. Fee makes this point with his characteristic force and vigor, *First Epistle*, 588.

28. I am pleased to commend to you the article by my friends McKirland, "Who's

act of inclusion and rectification, is central to the uniting of the church in 12:13 where the social hierarchies are excommunicated from the presence of God. Nothing in 1 Corinthians 12–14 suggests a pyramid of gender or socioeconomic status, but rather that the Spirit is the one who sovereignly and rightly grants gifts to the body for the sanctification of those who are in Christ. There is no place in Paul's mind for dishonoring those who are marginalized or subordinated within the church, and these deserve "greater honor" (τιμὴν περισσοτέραν: 12:23), not subordination. The church is not a place where people are torn down and dehumanized.[29] Instead, the body of Christ is a place that elevates people to their full rights as daughters and sons of a holy God. Paul's response to this sort of theological segregation is to condemn it and chastise those who enacted it, like the apostle Peter earlier in Galatians. A central text that follows this tongue-lashing is found in Galatians 3:26–29:

> For you are all sons of God through faith in Jesus Christ. For as many of you who were baptized into Christ have been clothed by Christ. There is neither Jew nor Greek, there is neither slave nor free person, there is no male and female: for you are all one in Christ Jesus. And if you belong to Christ, then you are Abraham's offspring, heirs according to the promise.

The baptism of all members of society was the key act of solidarity with one's brother and sister, where the transformation of social boundaries begins the eventual dissolvement of the institution of slavery, economic exploitation, and sexism. When it comes to gender, Galatians 3:28 does not mean that women and men cease to be women and men. Rather, excluding women from full participation in the church because of their gender finds its support in preferentialism and chauvinism, not in Pauline theology. For some, pivoting to the idea of Galatians 3:28 being about soteriology[30] in order to dilute Paul's radical egalitarianism runs counter to the notion that Jews at the time of Paul did not believe that women, slaves, and other people from among the nations could be saved—that these three groups somehow needed an extra bit of grace or salvific mysticism. Or even, they needed an

---

in Charge?," 15–25.

29. Fee, *First Epistle*, 613–14. This text can also speak to those who have been marginalized by the church on the basis of sexuality or disability.

30. Johnson, "Role Distinctions," 148–60. To attribute this text to the realm of soteriology is to impoverish the social and personal elements of how soteriology works within our lives.

extra bit of atonement. To be as understated as possible, Judaism at the time of Paul was not so enmeshed in narcissism, sexism, and ethno-cynicism to believe such things. Baptism, faithfulness, and being an heir according to God's promises (Gal 3:28–29) means that one is conformed and integrated into God's new family, where partiality based upon race, class, and gender is removed and set outside of God's will.[31] As such, to exclude women from full participation in the church is contrary to the revealed will of God for human holiness. Male and female together represent the image of God, and one cannot support the exclusion of God's image and expect the church to survive. Instead, the act of Pentecost is Scripture's fundamental assertion of God's sovereign ability to impart gifts to whomever the Spirit desires (Acts 2:28). Paul, in being a good Trinitarian and by saying what he does throughout all of his Epistles concerning women and giftedness, is simply submitting to the sovereignty of the Holy Spirit by calling upon all Christians to act in accordance with their calling. The agency and sovereignty of the Holy Spirit is diminished or even denied when we exclude women from exercising what the Spirit has gifted them to do. Christian perfection assumes the equality of male and female as embodied creatures, striving together in partnership toward who they were created to be.

In Galatians 3:26–29 we see a unique vision of a diverse body of believers who are united to Christ, with equal placement and calling through the act of baptism in the Spirit (Eph 4:5). Full union with Christ is being baptized into his death (Rom 6:3–4; Col 2:12) with the hope and anticipation of participating in the kingdom of God-in-Christ in the new creation (2 Cor 5:16–17). The power and presence of the Spirit is where ecclesiology must be centered, and in this there is no distinction based on ontology, but only on the Spirit, who is an equal opportunity employer.[32] The ultimate objective of the Spirit is to present a people perfected to God, with sin being the entity cast entirely from their lives. Without partnership, there is no sanctification to be found.

4.3b: Women & Men in Vocational Partnership

For those who are called to be ministers and preachers of God's holy word, one is forced to consider the reality of making disciples (Matt 28:19–20)

---

31. Cutler, "New Creation," 21–29.

32. I cannot claim this phrase as my own. I believe, and I could be wrong, I originally heard it used by Ben Witherington III in a lecture.

and the purpose of making disciples. For the early church, there was a strong sense of urgency on the part of apostles and prophets to take the gospel into all areas of the Roman Empire. In Romans 16 we see a whole host of names—both men and women—at work in the church. The closest we get to a centralized hierarchy is the designation of Andronicus and Junia[33] as "prominent among the apostles" in Romans 16:7. This is because no other apostle is named in Romans aside from Paul (1:1; 11:13), and hence, these two are the ones who likely founded the church. If Junia is Joanna from Luke's Gospel, then we have a direct eyewitness to the resurrection of Jesus[34] and a female apostle in the earliest strata of the beginning of Christianity.[35] Together with the women and men throughout Romans 16, we see an organic community functioning to perform and live out the gospel without any notion of hierarchy. Phoebe is the one who provided Paul with patronage (16:2) and Priscilla and Aquila risked their necks for Paul's own life (Rom 16:4). Women and men working together in vocational leadership is not a foreign issue for Paul because it flows directly out of his gospel conviction: God is working to redeem all creation and all of humanity is invited to participate in this cosmic act.[36] Paul also directly greets a woman in Philemon 2 (Apphia), suggesting her leadership and status in the church.[37] Similarly, in Philippines 4:2–3 we have multiple women and men as "co-workers" without any hint of their preferentialism.[38] As agents of sanctification, the early church was united in this mission to reconcile all things to God through the empowerment of the Spirit. Without men and women working in gifted partnership to achieve this goal, the church will be reviled and ineffective in its pursuit of discipleship and formation.

---

33. Cervin, "A Note," 464–70.

34. Luke 8:3; 24:10. Paul's own explanation (1 Cor 15:1–8) leaves the women out, but we know the women witnessed the resurrected Jesus *before* the twelve disciples did. For the idea that Joanna is Junia, see Bauckham, *Gospel Women*, 165.

35. The notion of apostleship in Romans is defined as "one who is set apart by God" (Rom 1:1). As such, there is no reason to assert that Paul's apostleship is different from Junia's.

36. See Quient, "Paul's God."

37. Quient, "Was Apphia?"

38. Junia, Phoebe, and other women (and men) throughout Rom 16 are never reminded of their subordinate yet somehow equal status. Rather, their full participation is assumed in their gospel-centered work. Since many of them are also potentially slave names, this illustrates Paul's radical egalitarianism as it relates both to gender, class, and social status. Jewett, *Romans*, 961.

4.3c: Excursus: "Restrictive Texts" on Women in Ministry

In my mind, only two texts of Paul can be wielded to exclude women from exercising ordained ministry: 1 Corinthians 14:34–35 and 1 Timothy 2:12. The history of interpretation concerning these two verses has resulted in the exclusion of women from ordained ministry—the female as female is excluded because she is female, and this is an issue that I believe has hindered the church. I know numerous women who are barred from pastoral ministry on the basis of their gender, and even women who are granted ministerial authority often have incredible barriers placed around them—this is not how it was intended to be. As a man who has learned from some remarkable female pastors and New Testament scholars like Dr. Love L. Sechrest and Dr. Marianne Meye Thompson, I find it biblically indefensible to exclude them and other women from the calling with which God has clearly gifted them. In my own upbringing, I believed that certain texts excluded women from ordained ministry, and I appealed to them often. As an evangelical Christian, I must affirm what Scripture says, so these texts deserve some brief consideration. The first text to be considered (1 Cor 14:34–35) is textually suspect according to many textual critics,[39] as these two verses appear after v. 40 in certain manuscripts,[40] and are a gloss likely added later in Codex Vaticanus.[41] Hence, it is difficult to say with certainty that these two verses were originally in 1 Corinthians, and so anyone who appeals to them as a foundational paradigm to exclude women is on deeply shaky ground. When we come to 1 Timothy 2:12 this question is somewhat different. There are no textual disturbances in 1 Timothy 2:12 to suggest that it was a later interpolation into the text, nor will it do to simply say Paul did not write the Pastoral Epistles—as I suspect Paul did write them. This places me within a minority position among other New Testament scholars, but I don't mind. The verse reads: "but I am not permitting a woman/wife to teach or to αὐθεντεῖν a man/husband. But she is to remain in quietness." Questions about whether this is about ecclesiology or a household is simply beyond the discussion, as both words for "husband" and "wife" can be translated as "man" and "woman." The untranslated Greek infinitive "assume authority" (αὐθεντεῖν) is a verb that has occasioned no small amount of scholarly debate. The verb could mean "exercise authority," "to

---

39. Fee, *First Epistle*, Revised ed., 782–92.
40. D F G 88*.
41. Payne, "A Summary."

assume authority," "to domineer," to "seize," or "wield control" of a husband/man.[42] This rare word is pesky—this is the only time it is used at all in the New Testament, and it occurs only once in the LXX (Wis 12:6) and once in Philo (*Quod deterius potiori insidiari* 1.78) in what appears to be a violent context. The most persuasive scholarly studies of this word are from Philip Payne, Cynthia Westfall, and Jamin Hübner, and they have all decisively demonstrated that Paul at the time of authoring the Pastoral Epistles was not permitting women to "seize control" or "wield control" over their husbands:[43] the very thing Paul warned against in 1 Corinthians 7:3–5. Paul's temporary prohibition[44] of women teaching heresy does not require us to force the entirety of his words about women elsewhere in the New Testament through the lens of 1 Timothy 2:12, nor does this require that we apply the same standard used with heretical women to gospel women who are clearly gifted, empowered, and called by the Spirit. The appeal to the "created order" (1 Tim 2:13–15) centers on Paul's biblical theological narrative: Eve, as a typological example (like Adam is in Rom 5:12), was deceived (Gen 3:12). Allison Quient has shown that this text functions similarly to Adam-Christ comparisons in relation to typology.[45] Women, and possibly men, in Ephesus were following after Eve's example and they are instead to "learn" (1 Tim 2:11): this posture is opposed to wielding self-asserted control over another.[46] They are not told to submit or withhold their gifts or put themselves beneath the notion of male authority. Rather, they are to learn how to be Christlike before acting unlike Christ. The weight of the evidence confirms that Paul's vision of baptism and holiness did not exclude women from exercising their gifts in teaching and admonishing others to be united to Christ. To exclude women from exercising the prophetic[47] gifts granted to them by God runs counter to the totality of Paul's theology

---

42. Hübner, "Revisiting Clarity."

43. Payne, *Man and Woman*, 291–398; Hübner, «Revisiting αὐθεντέω." For the most compelling reading of this section of 1 Timothy see Westfall, *Paul and Gender*, 279–312.

44. Paul's use of the present tense form of the verb "I am not permitting" makes best sense of this. Payne, *Man and Woman*, 319–37.

45. Allison M. Quient, "Eve Christology."

46. In addition to Payne and Westfall's work, see also Davis, "First Timothy 2:12."

47. To say that 1 Cor 11:2–16 subordinates or excludes women from exercising ministerial leadership functions in the church is a complete misreading, simply because women are expected to prophesy (11:5) and exercise their own "authority" (11:10). Biological distinctions between men and women do not logically require women's subordination to the vague preference of "male headship."

of sanctification, vocation, the Spirit, baptism, union with Christ, and the perfection of the person before a perfect God. It is to baptize and sanctify patriarchy instead of seeing it for what it is: a product of the fall and sin.

4.4: Conclusion

Sanctification, as it relates to God's original vision for humanity, must include the removal of all things that characterize this sinful age. Paul's apocalyptic perspective includes the renewal of creation, including the created order—and this applies to various notions of gendered hierarchy that have their genesis in the fall. The significance of entire sanctification as it relates to gender is that gender is not to be removed or decimated, but rather that creation's original intent was for the mutuality of the sexes, not their hierarchical ordering. As Cynthia Westfall has argued, "If women are led by the Spirit, then they are identified with the life and righteousness of Jesus Christ."[48] The doctrine of entire sanctification promotes the equal standing of men and women together as agents of the Spirit, emboldened by holiness to do good deeds in mutual partnership with one another. The destruction of Satan and all evil things are predicated upon the apocalyptic reality of God's encroaching kingdom; this includes the final annihilation of the sins of patriarchy, racism, and slavery. New creation (2 Cor 5:17) does not apply only to men—old creation and all the trappings of that sinful age are doomed to perish and have indeed begun to perish in the light of Advent. Egalitarian theology requires the mutual participation of person united by an equal and common goal: our perfection and conformation into Christ by the power of the Spirit. This process and journey must be done together in harmony with one another, and this does not permit the hierarchization of sanctification and glorification. Christians are now called to live life in light of the revelation of Christ and the Holy Spirit, not the decimated reality that was brought forth by Adam and Eve. This is not over-realized eschatology—it is biblical theology. Or rather, as Westfall says, "the notion that women were created to be subordinate fails to recognize that women's eschatological future must be consistent with their purpose at creation."[49] Genesis 1–3 presents us with a vision of shared leadership at the heights of divinely granted life; mutuality between Adam and Eve is the paradigm we are to imitate, not their destructive and fallen state that Christ has

---

48. Westfall, *Paul and Gender*, 129.
49. Westfall, *Paul and Gender*, 173.

overcome. This plays directly into entire sanctification and eschatology, and so this will be discussed in the next chapter rather extensively.

The calling of God to a life of service and ministry is not a calling to be accepted lightly. Whether by means of marriage or singleness, God is at work in the lives of all people, calling them toward God's self. The mission of the church is for the empowerment of her people, to disciple people in the ways of Jesus. The church is God's agent of sanctification and holiness, where the sins of this age are not permitted to exist. When the church is the church, the very act of participating in sanctification is the great act of holy resistance one can offer in this life. So, as ministers, we go forth and seek perfection together through the baptism of the Spirit for the glory of God.

5

In the End, God
Perfection & the Consummation of All Things

5.1: Reframing the Question of Hell

For many Christians, the question of the "end" of all things is ultimately a question about hell and suffering. Very little is usually said about what this "end" contains, only that this end consists of pain and anguish and a form of torment as it relates to evil. However, it must be said that Paul did not envision the "end" in a way where people and entities are kept alive forever and ever. Paul's vision of "hell" or the "end" must be reframed in broader and more precise ways. For the apostle, the question is not about whether God torments people forever and ever. Rather, the question should be seen as, "What is God's ultimate response to evil in the world?" How does God respond to injustice and violence and oppression and exploitation? Hence, theodicy is at the center of Paul's thought world as it relates to sanctification and God's ultimate act in response to the terrors that bind and enslave us. This reconceptualization will press us toward a more robust biblical theology that takes seriously the evils of our world and God's ultimate answer to our terrors and our trials. Apocalyptic theology or eschatology cannot be projected into the future, as if God is not at work now in our world to redeem and wage a cosmic battle against evil. Apocalyptic eschatology is a present reality where God is focused on liberation *now* through the church and by the power of the Holy Spirit. The resurrection is God's ultimate apocalyptic act in Christ and hence all Christian theology must reckon with the living Jesus and what this Jewish Messiah accomplished.

Therefore, Paul is a pastor struggling with the question of God and evil throughout his Epistles, and that is a central concern for our world. Sanctification as perfection is thus a major interpretive element that must infiltrate our conversations about any notion of apocalyptic "wrath" or "punishment."

5.2: The Sanctification of Creation as Corporate Liberation in Romans 8

Paul's words in Romans 8:18–23 are an appropriate lens by which we begin our conversation. The text reads as follows:

> [18]For I think that the sufferings of the present time are not worthy to compare to the coming glory to be apocalyptically disclosed to us. [19]Because the created order is eagerly waiting with anticipation for the revealing of the sons of God, [20]for creation was subjected with frustration, not willingly, but because of the one who subjected it in hope [21]that even creation itself would be emancipated from its enslavement of destruction for the freedom of the glory of the children of God. [22]For we know that all creation has joined together in groaning and suffers the pain of childbirth until now. [23]And not only this but also we ourselves—the ones who possess the first-fruits of the Spirit—groan amongst ourselves, anticipating adoption as sons,[1] the emancipation of our bodies.

All of creation is subjected to turmoil and anguish and the evidence of this can be found on whatever news channel you prefer: wars, rumors of wars, violence, racism, oppression, and degradation rule over this present evil age. The present reality of suffering and anguish is a prime element of Christian thought, although the notion of escapism is to be ignored. For Paul in Romans 8:18–23 we see an active reality—the created order—responding to corruption and the process of destruction, where the cosmos is cognizant of its own status and anguish amidst corruption and degradation. However, the hope of "emancipation" is something the corrupted reality anticipates in response to the Christ event. Sanctification—the act of pursuing holiness—lies behind the cosmology of Paul's statements here,

---

1. Here, Paul is addressing a mixed audience and hence women (and slaves!) are included with the status of first-born sons.

similar to how he speaks of perfecting holiness elsewhere (2 Cor 7:1). There is an ecological distinction to be made: humanity is called to participate in sanctification as agents of Christ, but creation itself has no specific call. Rather, creation is in need of liberation by means of humanity and our work as agents of liberation. God's own hope for a liberated cosmos (Rom 8:20–21) is set in opposition to agents of destruction and corruption, who seek to subordinate and dominate the created realm. God's act of subordination is assumed to be for the benefit of the oppressed, with the ultimate goal of "adoption" and "emancipation." Thinking ecclesiologically and ecologically, the church is to be God's agent of redemption in a world beset by violence and horror. The church is united to this cosmic reality and we participate with it, groaning and eagerly anticipating and even suffering *with* the created order. The goal of glory is the final culmination of perfection in God's cosmic order, where sin and evil are ultimately removed from all reality. God's process of rectification assumes a new reality (Gal 6:15; 2 Cor 5:17) where the kingly image of the eternal Son is supreme above all other orders and realities and principalities and sovereignties (Col 1:15–20). God's perfection of the cosmos is the ultimate restoration of the original design in creation and Eden.

The Adamic and Evenic[2] reality cannot be maintained if God is both sovereign and good and active, willing to respond in defiance of the invasion of evil. The sanctification of people means the sanctification of creation, which includes redemption and rectification. There can be no rival orders or sovereign realities outside of God, and Paul's apocalyptic vision of entire sanctification includes the final cessation of all evil things outside of God's good will.

- 5.2a: When Evil is Undone: The Final Annihilation of the Sovereignties

When it comes to various aspects of sanctification, we have seen the positive aspirations of what this doctrine entails. For this section, we are forced to consider what happens when a person refuses to participate in the work of God-in-Christ. What happens to those who refuse to align themselves with the reign of God? What happens to those who proclaim allegiance to the sovereignty of death and sin? Numerous ideas have been professed throughout the great tradition of Christian history. Many theologians have postulated a form of purgation where a person is purified and ultimately redeemed. Because human freedom is required for the completion

---

2. Yes, I made up a word.

of this process, one cannot affirm, with any sense of dogmatic certainty, universalism.[3] Others, sometimes in combination with this idea, affirm a view of universalism where the human person is ultimately reconciled to God, either through the fire or through the work of the Son, or even both.[4] Others propose what is called "conditional immortality" or "annihilationism," the belief that all that is wicked is destroyed including the soul/body of the human person.[5] The mainstream report throughout church history is decidedly against such views, almost always promoting the idea of the eternal torment of the wicked in a place called "hell," usually presented in conjunction with the idea of the immortality of the soul. For our purposes, I believe the best exegetical case resides within the conditional immortality or annihilationist perspective, and I will illustrate that this was Paul's view concerning the end of all evil, including those who have willfully aligned themselves with the powers.[6] This must be argued on the basis of everything this book has suggested beforehand, and I am especially eager to see how Christian perfection applies to various elements of apocalypticism and eschatology.

Several key texts directly address the problem of the end of evil in Paul's thought. For the sake of clarity, I will categorize them under two specific groups: first, the demonic or conceptual powers, and second, human agents. I am doing so, not because I believe the fate of both groups are in tension—indeed I think the fate of both is their utter termination—but the goal is to be as nuanced as possible.

5.2b: The Destruction of Satan in Romans 16:20

In an often-disregarded verse, Paul outlines the specific end of a principal agent in the rebellion against God: Satan. Paul writes

> But the God of peace will crush (συντρίψει) Satan beneath your feet in swiftness. The grace of our Lord Jesus Christ be with you.

---

3. Walls, *Purgatory*.

4. Talbott, *Inescapable Love*. MacDonald, *Evangelical Universalist*.

5. Fudge, *Fire that Consumes*.

6. The purpose of this section is not to argue specifically *against* a given view, but rather to illustrate how Paul's logic supports the idea of the utter eradication of evil as it relates to the "end."

What is compelling about this verse is that it directly matches the fate of Satan that is proclaimed elsewhere in Scripture (Heb 2:14–15): as the principal evil actor in the divine drama, Satan maintains a significant presence in the New Testament. The language Paul uses in this text is fascinating on two accounts. First, the language of being placed "under your feet" suggests destruction (Ps 109:1 LXX),[7] and the church is the agent in doing this. Second, the rather violent verb συντρίψει is used throughout Second Temple literature to denote destruction, especially as it relates to warfare. Similar texts found in 1 Maccabees 4:32 and 2 Maccabees 12:28 are specific in their vision of the "destruction" of their enemies: "but they called upon the Sovereign who with great power shatters (συντρίβοντα) the might of his enemies" (2 Macc 12:28). The book of Odes also speaks of "The Lord shattering (συντρίβων) [enemies in] wars" (1:3; 7:44),[8] a view that is also echoed in Judith 9:7 and 16:2. In Judith specifically, God is the specific agent who "crushes" or "destroys" various warriors and nations who rebel against God. This suggests linguistic and thematic continuity with Romans 16:20 and that Satan's fate is utter decimation, where there is no life, vitality, or existence. Hence, the final end of Satan in Pauline thought coordinates best with the view that those who participate in evil against God's call to participate in sanctification and victory in Christ will ultimately be undone in death (Rom 6:23).

5.2c: The Destruction of Death in 1 Corinthians 15:24–26

Paul's apocalyptic magnum opus in 1 Corinthians 15:24–26 reads as follows

> [24] *Then the final End: when he hands over the Kingdom to God, even the Father, after he has annihilated all rulership and all sovereignty and power* [25] *For he will continue to reign until he has placed all of the adversaries beneath his feet.* [26] *The final enemy to be utterly annihilated is Death.*

These verses in the larger pericope of 1 Corinthians 15:20–28 represent a master vision where Paul outlines in some detail what will happen to all evil things, particularly the fate of the powers and the sovereignties. The

---

7. Specifically, the language of "corpses" (πτῶμα) and and the verb for "shattering" (συνθλάω) in Psalm 109:5–6 of the LXX denote annihilation. This victory is envisioned as a military conquest, not a passive or peaceful submission.

8. The verb can also be used to denote metaphorical destruction: see Sir 13:2 and 27:2.

notion of dueling sovereignties is a question that Paul has wrestled with throughout his entire surviving corpus: Jesus the Lord vs. Caesar and the empires of this world—and the problem of compelling imperial ideologies in the ancient world—are finally confronted here. Christ's kingship is predicated upon his sole exercise of sovereignty and the annihilation of all (πᾶσαν) of the universal realities that have shaped the cosmos; nothing evil has escaped Christ's grasp. A key Greek verb bookends our section here (v. 24: καταργήσῃ in relation to the annihilation of the powers) and in the complete annihilation (v. 26: καταργεῖται) of the final enemy.[9] These realities (the powers) and the final enemy (death) will cease to be when Christ finally and decisively acts in response to their tyranny. Similarly, the various "rulers" will also be "destroyed" or "brought to nothing"[10] (καταργουμένων) in 1 Corinthians 2:6. Thiselton notes, "The present tense underlines that they are in the process of being reduced to nothing; this process remains continuous as an unstoppable process, i.e., they are doomed to come to nothing, or doomed to pass away."[11] The perfection of creation and the call for holiness means that the current world order is in direct conflict with God's desires. God's will for a world without sin is predicated upon the free actions of creatures who refuse God's gift of Christ, and all who have aligned themselves with the sovereignties will be given over finally into death.[12] The hostility of the powers—both human and non-human—is doomed to nothingness, as sin cannot co-exist with God and God's people in the new creation. This word group (καταργέω) is also applied to the "lawless one" or the "person of lawlessness" (ὁ ἄνθρωπος τῆς ἀνομίας) in 2 Thessalonians 2:7-10. In response to the evil done by this figure, Jesus will "kill" (ἀνελεῖ) him and "annihilate" (καταργήσει) him when he comes in glory (2 Thess 2:8).[13] To be more precise, Paul's use of ἀνελεῖ reflects what Cain did to Abel (4 Macc 18:11): that is, the result of human agency brings forth death toward other human beings.

---

9. Louw-Nida glosses this verb as "to cause to cease to exist - 'to cause to come to an end, to cause to become nothing, to put an end to.'" 13.100.

10. Richard Hays observes the following: "this parallel [with 1:28] shows that it is God who is acting to destroy these rulers and to establish his sovereignty over the world." *First Corinthians*, 43.

11. Thiselton, *First Epistle*, 231–32.

12. Regardless if the sovereignties comprise human or metaphoric or demonic forms (or varying aspects of some or all of these), their final end is annihilation.

13. Isa 11:4 LXX speaks of God "kill[ing]" the wicked as well.

The discontinuity produced by sin and death in God's cosmos means that Paul's vision of a triumphant God entails the annihilation of all things hostile to God; the final enemy of God is that which seeks to dominate all of creation, this ultimate adversary—death. The removal of sin from the body of the believer (Rom 6:6) echoes the removal of sin and evil from the cosmic order here. In responding to the created powers, God renders them null and void, with utter decimation and final obliteration for the benefit of those who were oppressed by them and enslaved to them.

5.3: The Silence Over the Waters: Paul & the Destruction of Evil

As Jesus will slay the "lawless one," so too this fate indicts those who have professed allegiance to him. Paul writes in 2 Thessalonians 2:10 that there are some who "refuse[d] love and truth so as to be saved." Their fate is "destruction" (ἀπολλυμένοις).[14] This is echoed in 2 Thessalonians 1:9 where "eternal destruction" (ὄλεθρον αἰώνιον) comes from the apocalyptic Lord, ending their rebellion. Paul's blatant echo of Isaiah 2:10–21 LXX denotes the encroachment of YHWH[15] in asserting violent and irrevocable judgment upon God's enemies.[16] Though people are attempting to separate themselves from God into the rocks of the hills, YHWH cannot be escaped from nor can YHWH permit their separation; justice demands God's response and God responds with utter decimation. This basically flies in the face of exegesis that asserts that Paul here in 2 Thessalonians 1:9 is speaking of "separation," when the context and intertext are specific: those who try to escape will suffer the punishment of eternal destruction, not separation.[17] The preposition ἀπὸ does not refer to separation; instead, the preposition communicates the source of the judgment, the immanent God from whom one cannot escape. Additionally, Paul applies that divine activity to Jesus, attributing the final and violent end of oppressive people to his apocalyptic

---

14. The tense form also denotes the process of their destruction, the same as how Paul has described this activity in 1 Cor 1:28 and 2:6 above.

15. Quient, "Destruction."

16. In his entire surviving corpus, Paul never speaks of the eternal torment or continual agony of people or powers who are hostile to God.

17. There is a certain level of irony in public discussions about the "nature" of hell, but the clear point of this text is that while some are trying to escape (i.e., separate themselves from the apocalyptic God), they will be unable to do so in either the Isaiah text or Paul's Epistle.

appearance.¹⁸ For those who are in the process of being destroyed (1 Cor 1:18; 2 Cor 2:15), there will be no eternal life apart from repentance and faithful allegiance to Christ.¹⁹

Similarly, Paul's response to evil is to assert that the end of those who participate in sin have their "end in destruction" (ὧν τὸ τέλος ἀπώλεια) in Philippians 3:19. Two keywords need to be addressed as he presses on. The τέλος word group has been discussed above in sufficient detail and it carries a sense of finality in this context when paired with "destruction" (ἀπώλεια).²⁰ In Second Temple Jewish literature this word often has violent connotations as it relates to warfare and destruction (Jdt 6:4; 1 Macc 1:30; 3:42; 11:18; Wis 18:5). For Paul, the final end of those who persist in hostile insurrection against God will be removed entirely from all creation. In the end, the final realm of evil and death wages its final onslaught against God, only to suffer its final decimation. That is when God definitively puts to an end all hostilities and sovereignties, whether thrones, or dominions, or rulers, or people who have united themselves to such realities. In essence, the fate of Satan and the powers are intrinsically tied to the fate of those who have pledged fidelity to them: destruction. The consistency of Paul's theology demands the eradication of all evil things from creation; otherwise, the exercise of God's sovereignty remains compromised as well as his goodness and holiness. In the end, there will be silence over the waters and chaos will be no more. Creation will cease to be exploited, humanity will be liberated from the bondage of corruption, chaos, and evil, and perfection will reign over the totality of the created order.

5.4: Immortality & Perfection as Sanctification

The sobering reality of the final abolition of evil presses us to consider the character and attributes of God in light of this apocalyptic reality. Three

---

18. The word used for "destruction" never refers to "torment" or individualized "agony." Rather, throughout Jewish literature, it refers metaphorically or literally to the destruction of a person or a city or nation or empire. See Jer 48:8; 51:55.

19. "Destruction" is an outworking of the unethical heart and life, and eternal life is the product of a life and heart lived in the Holy Spirit (Gal 6:8). If the heart turns to ash, the whole person will inevitably succumb to the same fate.

20. The New Testament use of ἀπώλεια when applied to human agents suggests destruction and often has a violent connotation. See Louw-Nida: to destroy or to cause the destruction of persons, objects, or institutions - 'to ruin, to destroy, destruction'" (Matt 7:13; 10:28).

key terms are used throughout Paul's Epistles to describe this apocalyptic reality. They are "imperishability, incorruptibility" (ἀφθαρσία), "imperishable" (ἄφθαρτος), and "immortality" (ἀθανασία). All three words are similar yet distinct. The first word, ἀφθαρσία, refers to "a state of not being subject to decay, leading to death - 'immortal, immortality.'"[21] More specifically, this word refers to the idea of "being incorruptible." The second word is ἄφθαρτος and this word is more specific in reference to "being not subject to decay or death."[22] The final word ἀθανασία is more generic, referring to the state of being "immortal."[23] Paul uses these various words in a nuanced way that demands close scrutiny, but I believe they speak specifically to our thesis of Christian perfection.

5.4a: The Attributes of the Immortal God

Throughout his letters, Paul ascribes several of these keywords to God. In Romans 1:23 he speaks of the "immortal" or "imperishable God (τοῦ ἀφθάρτου θεοῦ) in contrast to "perishable humanity" (φθαρτοῦ ἀνθρώπου). The distinction Paul draws between the created order and the one who created the totality of all reality is sharp: ἀφθάρτου vs. φθαρτοῦ, suggesting a distinction of quality. That is, God as Creator is imperishable or unable to be tainted or touched by corruption and death, whereas humanity is subjected to such things as creation is.[24] This language occurs throughout Philo's corpus to suggest a distinction between God and creation,[25] as well as Second Temple literature to describe the attributes of God as "imperishable/immortal" (Wis 12:1; 18:4). God is not subject to the mortality and perishability of the cosmos, which implies that God is the source and sustainer of all creation. Hence, God and God alone possesses the attribute of "deathlessness." Similarly, in the Pastoral Epistles we see this sort of language being applied to God. First Timothy 1:17 addresses the "incorruptible" (ἀφθάρτῳ) and "unseen" (ἀοράτῳ) God alone, attributing honor and glory and praise to God[26] and God's kingdom.[27] Christ's own attributes are

21. Louw-Nida 23.127.
22. BDAG 1076.
23. BDAG 120.
24. Jewett, *Romans*, 160.
25. *De opficio mundi* 1:82 and 1:119.
26. Marshall, *Pastoral Epistles*, 405.
27. While it may be true that Paul intends to include only God the Father here per

included as Christ is the source of belief and "eternal life" (1:16), pressing the activity of God-in-Christ ever closer together. The spatial and terrifying aspect of God's own presence is highlighted strongly in 1 Timothy 6:16. Paul asserts that God alone possesses "immortality" (ἀθανασίαν) as an exclusive attribute. Humanity at the present does not possess any of these three specific related attributes, and these attributes are conferred upon the resurrection of the righteous and the righteous alone.[28] Finally, Paul's apocalyptic vision in 2 Timothy 1:10 is predicated upon the apocalyptic appearance of Jesus who is casting death down from its high place and "destroying" (καταργήσαντος) it. This was done as Christ manifested the new reality of "life and immortality" (ζωὴν καὶ ἀφθαρσίαν) by means of his gospel. We cannot forget the interplay between life and immortality, as both describe aspects of God's new creation in imparting continuance of life to all who are faithful to Christ. We cannot attribute the destruction of death exclusively to God or to Christ, but only to both as is fitting for Father and Son together producing life over and against the power and sovereignty of death. For Paul, God is sovereign and separate from the created order, but not detached and unwilling to invite creation to participate in glory and honor and immortality. God's eschatological glory is inevitably moving toward perfection, where the cosmos is indeed finally and irrevocably purified of all sin and death. Then, all will be like God.

5.4b: Immortality & the Human Person

To assert that God and God alone is immortal, incorruptible, imperishable is to assert God's sovereignty over the totality of the cosmos. The possession and actualization of immortality as something that can be conferred upon others illustrates an immense dignity in revealing God's eternal benevolent disposition toward creation. God gets to choose who lives into eternity with him and the means of this are most prominently displayed in Romans 2:7: "to those who in accordance with perseverance (ὑπομονὴν) in doing good works by seeking glory and honor and incorruptibility (ἀφθαρσίαν), he will give eternal life (ζωὴν αἰώνιον)." Two things are immediately clear and unavoidable: first, humanity is to "seek" after the things of God. Second, if

---

the comments by Towner, *Letters to Timothy*, 152, it cannot be said that God the Son is excluded as King of the kingdom (Eph 5:5).

28. This is most vividly stated in 1 Cor 15:42–55 where "corruption" is destroyed by God's empowering Spirit in making us "incorruptible."

they do so, they will be gifted that which can only come from God, and that is life eternal. Paul's logic is intricate and precise: humanity is granted "imperishability" by active and faithful allegiance to God, yet God is the source of this "imperishability" and "eternal life." Good works that illustrate the vocation of holiness make manifest the life of the person in her professed action toward Christ. This is a symbol of "incorruptible" (ἀφθαρσίᾳ) love toward the Lord Jesus Christ (Eph 6:24) as affection. Titus 2:7 is similarly explicit: "in all things show yourself to be a model of good works in teaching, incorruptibility (ἀφθορίαν), holy dignity." The human person is shown what is good and righteous before God and what God requires of that person: holiness. Holiness is the goal of the Christian life, and perfect holiness is not something to be downplayed or disregarded; holiness by the Spirit is a reality that infuses all of the person's life. The calling to forsake all evil and be united to Christ marks our lives, and our bodies are examples of this holy reckoning. Our bodies and the desire for emancipation from sin and death mark the spirit of the believer.

In the end, in our entire sanctification, death dies.

5.5: Conclusion: Death is Undone

In tying all three of these threads together, we see several rather striking points. We see that the principal powers of this cosmic order are not long for existence. God is at work in Christ to destroy all evil from creation. Hence, the parallel existence of a cosmos that is free from sin, corruption, and bondage mirrors the predicament of the human person. However, the future incorruptibility of the body is not predicated upon Christian perfection or entire sanctification, nor is creation contingent upon human agents being perfected by the Spirit in this life. Indeed, the necessity of the human person in being entirely sanctified by the Holy Spirit reveals that God's call is missional and ecological and communal in responding to the terrors of our world. Rather, the continuity of the event of sanctification would be long established by the resurrection of the body. The resurrection event assures us that if a person has not been entirely sanctified before his or her death, the process will continue onward until it is achieved in Christ. At the basest level of human existence, there lies triumph despite the terror and the present calamity.

The triumph of God's final victory is in the disclosing of grace in the invasive power of holiness that threatens the dominion of this present order. God's gift of sanctification in its entirety is the initial assault against evil. Where holiness is, there is treason against sin and death. Faith is not merely a mental assent to the proposition that Jesus is the resurrected Lord: faith is the allegiant covenantal love we show to Jesus by living our lives in the shadow of his lordship. Faith is the ignition that empowers the Christian life into the journey of godliness and by God's grace; the human person is not abandoned to wantonness and degradation. The bodies of men and women in Christ are thus redeemed—not of their distinctiveness or their stories—but of that which has plagued them since the beginning.

Christian perfection is, therefore, an apocalyptic and intrusive act of the Holy Spirit in the life of a called person, to be all that God has called her to be. The destruction of evil and the gift of eternal life confirm the participatory nature of the God-human relationship: that God would deign to become human like us in every way (Heb 2:14–15) so that we might be united fully to Christ by faith. Entire sanctification is the utter repudiation of evil and exemplifies God's work in us as we seek to be one in Christ (Gal 3:26–29). God has broken the back of the powers and we long for our day of liberation and for the resurrection unto eternal glory. Through all of the pain and turmoil of this present reality, there is hope in the reconciliation of all things. Until that blessed day, until that blessed time, we as embodied creatures must persist in faithfulness to Christ.

6

Answering Questions & Objections to Christian Perfection

We have surveyed the perfection of the incarnate Christ and how incarnational perfection impacts the human person in her totality. In learning about who Christ is, we can now see how the life of the eternal Son has a teleological orientation: a goal or purpose. Sanctification, as such, is an apocalyptic reality where God is at work in a divided and warring cosmos. When it comes to considering or affirming that doctrine of entire sanctification in the life of the Christian, one can scarcely affirm the view without considering various scholarly demurrals and questions concerning preaching and counseling this often-misunderstood doctrine. Thus, the first purpose of this chapter is to answer various objections made by theologians and biblical scholars and provide plausible responses to their oppositions. The second purpose is the most important part of this work for me personally, and that is answering various questions about pastoral ministry and practical applications. As someone who is an associate pastor and serves in a local congregation, I am tasked with the responsibility to respect and engage with various questions and insights that my brothers and sisters have, and if this doctrine cannot withstand their scrutiny, then this work is right to be proclaimed as a failure. For myself, I am less interested in theological and academic objections to my view than I am with people I serve with in church and their own questions and insights. If a person cannot live out this idea, then this book is a worthless spectacle.[1] The church and her questions and formation are of central concern to me in this quest for theological nuance. Therefore, I will deal with major theological objections to the doctrine of entire sanctification first and then spend the rest of this chapter answering possible questions church people may have.

6.1: Theological Dissenters to Entire Sanctification

While I do not believe that the doctrine of entire sanctification carries with it anything that a Reformed theologian could not affirm, nevertheless several popular objections are offered from the Reformed side of the Christian family.

6.1a: R. C. Sproul

What Sproul, may he sleep in peace, said deserves to be quoted in full:

> I once encountered a young man who had been a Christian for about a year. He boldly declared to me that he had received the "second blessing" and was now enjoying a life of victory, a life of sinless perfection. I immediately turned his attention to Paul's teaching on Romans [7]. Romans [7] is the biblical death blow to every doctrine of perfectionism. My young friend quickly replied with the classic agreement of the perfectionist heresy, namely, that in Romans [7] Paul is describing his former unconverted state. I explained to the young man that it is exegetically impossible to dismiss Romans [7] as the expression of Paul's former life. We examined the passage closely and the man finally agreed that indeed Paul was writing in the present tense. His next response was, "Well, maybe Paul was speaking of his present experience, but he just hadn't received the second blessing yet."[2]

Sproul also writes,

> The peril of perfectionism is that it seriously distorts the human mind. Imagine the contortions through which we must put ourselves to delude us into thinking that we have in fact achieved a state of sinlessness. Inevitably[3] the error of perfectionism breeds

1. But what a spectacle it is!
2. Sproul, "Heresy of Perfectionism."
3. This sort of rhetorical frontloading is unfortunate, given that Sproul offers no

one, or usually two, deadly delusions. To convince ourselves that we have achieved sinlessness, we must either suffer from a radical overestimation of our moral performance or we must seriously underestimate the requirements of God's law. The irony of perfectionism is this: though it seeks to distance itself from antinomianism, it relentlessly and inevitably comes full circle to the same error.[4]

Two things may be true at once. First, it is possible that a young man might be quite arrogant in his zeal and second, that R. C. Sproul has both mischaracterized the doctrine of entire sanctification and appealed to an unsustainable prooftext. First, it is not "we" who "achieve sinlessness." Rather, it is the power of the Holy Spirit at work in us. If one presupposes a Trinitarian reading of perfection, then one simply cannot assert that it is the sole priority of the human person. Indeed, especially within the doctrine of synergism, because of God's work and grace one has no room for boasting. Rather, it is a relational outworking of the Trinity in abundant love and patience with the human person, perfecting and purifying their will in light of the Spirit's guidance.

Sproul's rather surface appeal to Romans 7 is misguided as it does not account for multiple exegetical and rhetorical factors within Romans 7.[5] Sproul's comment "Romans 7 is the biblical death blow to every doctrine of perfectionism" is a statement that lacks specific exegesis to substantiate this rather polemical point. What Paul is doing in Romans 7 is continually debated,[6] and that ought to force a sense of humility upon all of us before engaging in theological virtue signaling. I suspect that Paul is using a rhetorical device called *prosopopoeia* or "speech-in-character,"[7] and is not speaking specifically about the "Christian" experience or even Paul's present experience. Paul has adopted an Adamic persona in Romans 7, and I strongly suspect that Paul has adopted the persona of Adam in Romans 7:7–13, rather than speaking of his own experience (that is, autobiographically). This can be argued on multiple points: Adam was mentioned rather strongly in Romans 5:12–21 and is the last historical figure to be

---

evidence for his assertion. This is simply a false sense of perilous assurance.

4. Sproul, "Heresy of Perfectionism."

5. For instance, how can Paul be alive without the law (Rom 7:9), or speak of his own death (7:10)?

6. See the rhetorical options cited in Greathouse and Lyons, *Romans 1–8*, 206.

7. Stowers, *Rereading of Romans*, 258.

spoken of, excluding Jesus. The "law" alluded to is "covetousness" or "lust" (ἐπιθυμήσεις) in v. 7b and in v. 8 the language of "commandment" (ἐντολῆς) suggests that Adam was told not to seek after/covet something: knowledge. More importantly, only Adam (and Eve) lived "apart" (χωρὶς) from the Law/ Torah: hence, this text is most likely Adam "speaking," being deceived (vv. 10–11),[8] and being the one who cries out "wretched human that I am, who will rescue me from this body of death?" (v. 24). The sphere of Adam/ mortality/ corruption is central to the assertion in Romans 8:1 that condemnation is gone for those who are in the sphere of Christ Jesus. Hence, far from being a "death blow" to entire sanctification, Romans 7 actually is quite coordinate with it, and entire sanctification might even be something that helps us reframe our doctrine of sin. The "performance" aspect is undone if one affirms the active work of the triune God in sanctification; Sproul's claim about "underestimate[ing] God's law" is an objection that will be dealt with below in response to Wayne Grudem.

However, even if others and I are wrong, that does not mean Sproul is correct to assert Romans 7 as the counter to Christian perfection. Indeed, the theology, rhetoric, and logic of Romans 7 are quite conducive to entire sanctification provided one can account for temporality and apocalyptic categories—as I believe I have shown thoroughly above. As Kenneth Collins has rightly noted, "We must, first of all, distinguish sanctification as a process (catholic element) that leads up to entire sanctification, from entire sanctification itself as an instantaneous actualization (protestant element) of grace."[9]

6.1b: Wayne Grudem

Theologian Wayne Grudem, in his *Systematic Theology*, has a brief response to the idea of entire sanctification. In offering a non-perfectionist reading of 2 Corinthians 7:1 (as well as other texts),[10] Wayne Grudem states the following objections: first,

8. You can find more precise argumentation in Witherington III and Hyatt, *Paul's Letter*, 188–90.

9. Collins, *Theology*, 293.

10. Grudem cites the aforementioned Matthean text and Corinthian text, 1 Thess 5:23, 1 John 1:8 and 3:6, 9 in his argument against "perfectionism." Most of these verses do not support his claim, but his citation (p. 752) of 1 John 1:8 carries some force. However, there are two objections: one, the negated present tense of ἔχομεν ("do not have") reveals a temporal reality: it simply states that the people within the Johannine community

> It is simply not taught in Scripture that when God gives a command, he also gives the ability to obey it in every case.

and second

> When Paul commands the Corinthians to make holiness perfect in the fear of the Lord or prays that God would sanctify the Thessalonians wholly (^{1} Thess $^{5:23}$), he is pointing to the goal that he desires them to reach. [Paul] does not imply that any reach it, but only that this is the high moral standard toward which God wants all believers to aspire.[11]

Three things must be noted by means of an initial response. First, one would not deny that Paul has in mind "the goal he desires them to reach" at all. In fact, I would affirm that. I just deny Grudem's conclusion, as I do not see it substantiated. A simple response I can give is that my exegesis above proves that the doctrine of entire sanctification is appropriate and biblical. The force of the participle in 2 Corinthians 7:1 must be taken into account, and Grudem fails to substantiate his objection. The exegesis of the various Pauline texts must be accounted for, not subsumed beneath various unstated theological constructs and a single text.

Second, when Grudem states, "[Paul] is pointing to the goal that he desires them to reach," he misunderstands the force of the verb. While it is true that Paul desires their "reaching" this goal, the Greek verb itself has more significance than Grudem allows, as I have already demonstrated above. The assertion of "attaining" the goal and desiring the goal is not a contradictory claim at all. If someone is told to seek after a goal with pneumatic intensity, it seems theologically suspect to believe that this goal is fundamentally unobtainable. To use an illustration, it is like telling a child to kick a soccer ball into the net, but you keep moving the net farther and farther away from the child so she cannot complete her goal. This appears both capricious and unnecessary based on the language and exhortation used to encourage her to kick the ball. It is difficult to accept, based on the biblical text that God is like this in any specific way. God may certainly

---

have not been perfect. Second, this is answered logically in the following chapter where there is an "advocate" who is a ἱλασμός for the sins of the whole world (1 John 2:2). So, 1:8 is a word of rebuke and a word of hope for those *presently* in sin. Grudem's argument, thus, has little force when the text is properly read in context: no Wesleyan would ever argue that all people are instantaneously converted to "perfection" upon participation in Christ. "If" we sin is indeed contingent upon a person sinning (1 John 2:1–2).

11. Grudem, *Systematic Theology*, 750–51.

use difficult situations for our growth and sanctification, but God certainly does not need to *cause* such events.

Third and finally, it seems unbiblical and counter intuitive that God would give a command that he does not desire for us to fulfill—this appears to place a form of duplicity upon God that is not warranted by a careful reading of the text. Additionally, this specific objection to the perfectionist reading of this verse assumes an unstated hermeneutical grid that appears foreign to Scripture.[12] As the analogy above has shown, the intent of God is for a people to conform to the image of his Son—why would he keep them from fulfilling the very thing he has called them to be? God's commands in Scripture are not given haphazardly; they are commands that can be fulfilled—provided one is faithful and in the Spirit.[13] The presence of sin in the lives of various Christians in the first century does not overturn my exegesis. It simply illustrates that point that some number of Christians had not yet been perfected at the time of Paul penning his various Epistles. Indeed, the teleological nature of the story of Christian salvation seems to press against such a notion as we saw in Paul's own descriptions in Philippians 3:12–15: the journey of holiness is part of the sanctifying process. Hence, when Sproul and others say we "underestimate God's law," one is forced to pause and then ask *how*? Those who affirm entire sanctification are taking God's law so seriously that we believe we can, by the power of the Holy Spirit, actually *do* God's law! Grudem's rather shocking comment, "It is simply not taught in Scripture that when God gives a command, he also gives the ability to obey it in every case" undoes the entire moral reasoning about why God gives laws in the first place. If one assumes that God is free to respond to human agents and nuance or qualify the law, that is appropriate; but to assert what Grudem does entirely undoes the entire nature of the Greek language as it relates to imperatives and Paul's ethical discourses.[14] If God wants us to do something, I think God will give us the means to

12. Grudem also cites Jas 3:2, but he is incorrect to do so: the Greek word πταίομεν ("stumble") does not necessarily coordinate with the language of "sin" (ἁμαρτία). In fact, this very verse reveals a perfectionistic reality since οὗτος τέλειος ἀνήρ is a consequence of a person "not being at fault." A person is able to "bridle" (χαλιναγωγῆσαι) their body, revealing an ability or power (δυνατὸς) to abstain from sin. So Grudem is mistaken to utilize this prooftext.

13. For those concerned with the First Testament saints, the Law was sufficient to fulfill God's purpose. I also believe the Spirit was active in the call to holiness during that time.

14. It also challenges the notion of divine simplicity and other attributes of classical theism.

achieve that. Sometimes it is that simple. The temporal presence of sin does not logically necessitate the eternal presence of sin in the life of the believer.

6.1c: Millard Erickson

Calvinist theologian Millard Erickson appeals to Romans 7 in support for the idea of non-perfection,[15] although he is more nuanced in recognizing the prima facie biblical support for entire sanctification. However, Erickson's argument falters when he says that "[Romans 7] appears to be a vivid and forceful testimony to the effect that the believer is not free from sin."[16] What is striking about this sort of objection is that on the one hand, other Wesleyans and I can affirm it wholeheartedly in part: *if* Romans 7 does indeed teach what Erickson says—and it is highly doubtful that it does—then yes, Paul is speaking about himself at the present time. But, as Erickson does not point out, one is free to ask about what happens *after* we keep reading on into Romans 8 and following. The present existence of sin is the present reality for all who are converted and baptized into Christ, but it does not follow that the Spirit cannot perfect someone if the Spirit chooses. Indeed, it seems to be a proper understanding of Paul's theology that the effect of the Holy Spirit is powerful enough to transform us into the likeness of Christ. Erickson's objection is based largely on a misunderstanding of the *temporal* nature of sin in God's cosmic scheme and also appears to downplay the power of the Spirit, and so it should be rejected.[17] Sin is not an eternal part of new creation. Sin had a beginning and it has a definitive end, both in the life of the believer as well as the apocalyptic end when God in Christ destroys all evil. Portraying the Christian as presently in sin does not take into account the journey of the Christian with the Spirit. Not all who participate in Christ are granted the gift of perfection; however, all who participate in Christ will be delivered from their sin, in this life or the next. Temporal aspect as it relates to the immediate presence of sin does not negate the journey of sanctification unto divine glory: the absence of sin is made complete through the loving and perfective power of the Holy Spirit's work.

15. Erickson, *Christian Theology*, 901.
16. Erickson, *Christian Theology*, 901.
17. Erickson, without lexical or exegetical support, says that the "perfect/tion" word group means "complete." This is both somewhat true and also linguistically narrow. It also does not take into account the various passages above. *Christian Theology*, 902.

The rest of Erickson's objections fail to take the temporal (already/not yet) aspect of sin into account (p. 903), but his nuanced understanding presents us Wesleyans with a warm heart insofar as he has faithfully interacted with our view without polemics or exaggeration. This level of charitable interaction is something that should always be present among the community of faith, especially as it relates to Christian charity and communal belovedness. As a summarizing point, once someone takes the temporal aspect of sin into account regarding the New Testament, most of the major theological and biblical objections fall away.

6.1d: Conclusion

I hope I have illustrated the plausibility of the doctrine of entire sanctification in light of the objections of Sproul, Grudem, and Erickson. Their points about the temporal nature of sin in the life of the believer are to be acknowledged and taken into account. However, this objection, as well as the few others mentioned, does not do justice to the biblical evidence and the theological nuances offered by Wesleyan theologians. The call of Paul in 1 Thessalonians 5:24 is central to the divine will: "the one calling you is faithful, and he will do this." On the heels of the call to entire sanctification is the divine reality that encompasses humanity in our physical and mortal reality. The clash between dueling realities is a clash between the power of sin and the power of God, and the power of God is that which beckons and calls us to participation, not to subjugation. However, more practical questions arise out of the arguments of this book, and in many ways, these questions are more important. If one cannot live this doctrine out to the glory of God, then one is forced to wonder about the merits of this theological reality.

6.2: Pastoral Questions & Answers

Can I lose my perfection?

This is a very good question, and there are multiple answers I could give. Based on the evidence of the New Testament, I believe that human beings can forfeit their salvation (Heb 6:4–6); it suggests they can also forfeit the nature of entire sanctification. New Testament Scholar I. Howard Marshall has written rather extensively on the topic of apostasy,[18] and if one carries the same logic and applies such logic to the doctrine of entire sanctification/Christian perfection, then the loss of perfection would be entirely possible, although I cannot imagine how it would precisely occur. However, it must be noted rather strongly that Christian perfection/entire sanctification is not equivalent to one's salvation in Christ. A person could conceivably sin and thus fall back into a life of sinfulness—but this behavior can be forgiven, and rectification is certainly possible if one repents. I imagine this question is similar to the idea of "free will" in heaven or in new creation. It is certainly conceivable that one could be entirely sanctified by the Spirit so that the thought of sin would be removed entirely from their heart. This remains a question for moral philosophers and apt theologians to ponder. I would say that this sort of sanctification can be forfeited, but I cannot see how one would desire to sin when fully united to Christ. Such desire would have been conformed to Christ-like holy love.

How do I know if I have been perfected?

In some sense, there is a simple answer to this question: one would know they have been entirely sanctified if they no longer seek a life of sinfulness. Perhaps a man or woman no longer struggles with pornography, sexual immorality, or drugs and substance abuse. Perhaps the desire for such things has been alleviated. Often, entire sanctification can be witnessed after a period of time. I am an associate pastor and I have seen numerous people in their life forsake the sins of the past, becoming sanctified in Christ. This does not mean the desire is fully gone or removed (although in some instances I do believe it is), but it is to say that people—through the gift of time—are freed from the desire to sin and thus are sanctified. This would be evidence that the Spirit has sanctified the believer of these sinful desires, insofar as the Spirit participates in the spiritual life of the Christian to the point where our very experiences and nature are transformed into the image of Christ. As such, this doctrine is immeasurably tied both to the practice of community and the necessity of practical theology and discipleship. Another way to notice this climactic process is through the witness of the faith community around you. Of course, not everyone is going to say, "You have been perfected!" as if you suddenly begin to glow or float a few inches above the ground. But in some sense, many can attest to a significant moral

---

18. Marshall, *Kept by Power*.

change in your life to the point where you are a new creation in Christ. The sins of the past that enslaved you are not present, indeed, as you reflect upon this, pray about your past. What has the Spirit removed from you? I know, sitting in this coffee shop right here, that the Spirit has done some miraculous things without me ever realizing it until now. The question of assurance or self-awareness is also a factor: asking the Spirit to show you how you have grown in Christ and have put aside the body of sin and death is a good place to start. The life of entire sanctification is a life of holy love and especially holy prayer.

Asking the Holy Spirit to invade your life and bring your sinful desires to nothing is an excellent start. Only after a period of time and reflection hopefully, in a community of faith that is accepting, wise, and mature, can one reflect and recognize what the Spirit has done. Do not forsake the journey for the destination as it relates to what God is doing in your life. As someone who continually struggles with certain vices like impatience, this is a pertinent reminder for me as well. The power of prayer is the greatest weapon one can utilize. Thus, the attestation of the community of faith and of authentic self-reflection is a major part of knowing that you have been entirely sanctified by the Spirit.

Can entire sanctification result in spiritual arrogance?

The sad but truthful answer is, "Yes, absolutely." Many virtues in the Christian have the possibility of being corrupted and abused: grace can lead to antinomianism, for example. A selfish impulse can be masked by the appearance of holiness. However, the notion of arrogance insofar as it relates to someone trumpeting their "perfection" is something that is counterintuitive: why would someone who has been entirely sanctified then go about and boast in what the Spirit has done in their life? Hence the need for self-reflection and emotional and theological honesty as it relates to our struggles and trials in this life. Not everyone who is a Christian will be sanctified entirely before their death. The purpose, therefore, of entire sanctification is not to be a burden to others—rather it is to be a source of empowerment and life for those who are struggling. The Holy Spirit calls us into this reality and if we utilize such a gift for ourselves and for ourselves alone, we have grieved the Spirit and caused great division and destruction within the body of Christ. Arrogance has no place in sanctification because entire sanctification is a work entirely predicated upon the power of the Holy Spirit, with whom we cooperate to be united entirely to Christ.

Does God stop loving me if the Spirit never perfects me?

God's holy love is without hesitation or reservation. God loves everyone. God's love for fallen humanity is unquenchable in its effect and location. God does not love one less for not being perfect, simply because God takes human freedom into account. God does expect people to persist and profess allegiance to the Spirit, and this is what God desires most. If one does this, then they will be conformed to the image of Christ. God does not stop loving you if you fall or sin or make a mistake. Perfection is not the measure of God's universal love: it is the means by which we as Christians are freed to love one another. The righteousness of God for you is the body of Christ, broken for you. Forgiveness is never something that is far from you. Rather, forgiveness and rectification are yours, at any time, no matter the sin, no matter the desire—the Spirit forgives and there is atonement to be gifted to you if you humbly and sincerely repent. The journey of faith is a journey often fraught with sin and agony, and the Spirit does not expect instant perfection. The Spirit knows of your suffering and your failings. Do not be afraid, friend—for Christ has overcome your desires and your sin and your failings, and has a constant invitation for you to, again and again, participate in the life of holiness.

Is entire sanctification the same as the Eastern Orthodox view of theosis?

In some ways, yes. Randy L. Maddox has astutely pointed out

> That both the Eastern and Western theological traditions embody important, but partial, truths. From such a perspective, Wesley's theological program might be judged more positively. At the least, he could be honored as an eclectic who gathered disparate truths wherever he found them. More ambitiously, some have advanced the claim that he has forged a unique synthesis of these two major Christian traditions. If this latter claim is true, then Wesley's theology holds truly ecumenical promise.[19]

---

19. Maddox, "John Wesley," 29–53, 42.

While there indeed are differences between John Wesley's view and other Eastern Orthodox theologians, the differences are not so vast as to put Wesley beyond the ecumenical promised land. Indeed, Protestant theologians like Michael J. Gorman—who is a Methodist—have done substantial work on theosis and Pauline theology.[20]

Can entire sanctification lead to legalism?

Yes, and this is a serious issue that must be confronted. Numerous friends of mine have come out of Wesleyan or Pentecostal traditions where legalism was a cudgel to batter people into theological submission. Many of us struggle against the idea of legalism and fundamentalism, presented as a rigid construct of immovable ideals and impenetrable and unknowable realities. God is portrayed as a cosmic sniper, watching and waiting for someone to trip before he pulls the trigger. However, the vision that I have presented here, where entire sanctification is actualized by means of Holy Scripture has a different result—hopefully. For those who are seeking sanctification and union with Christ, there is a deep and restless hope for rectification by the Spirit. The power of prayer, whether personal or communal, accompanied with the public reading of Scripture often presents people with a chance to reflect and to pause. The doctrine of entire sanctification itself cannot lead to legalism, but the pursuit of union with Christ can lead people toward sinful activity. This, of course, must be abandoned wholesale and the pursuit of sanctification within the community of faith is for the communion of the body. Legalism cannot participate where the Spirit has claimed. Legalism as a social construct of fundamentalist proportions is an unnecessary and crippling paradigm that quenches the Spirit, and if the Spirit is at work in our lives to liberate us from sin and death, then there can be no legalism. The fruits of the Spirit preclude certain activities such as sexual immorality and violence and avarice. However, against other such things, there is grace.

---

20. Gorman, *Inhabiting*.

Conclusion
Preaching Holiness

> "And do not be conformed to this age, but transform yourselves in the renewing of your mind, for you to test yourselves about what the will of God is: what is good and well-pleasing and perfect (τέλειον)"
>
> —Romans 12:1–2.

The doctrine of entire sanctification is woven throughout Paul's theological tapestry. In light of everything that has been written above, Paul takes an entirely different approach from many contemporary theologies and denominations. Rather than being concerned with mere legalism or pleasing God, Paul's theology is centered on humanity's empowerment through the Holy Spirit—and this empowerment continues into the realm of sanctification and holiness. For the doctrine of entire sanctification to rise or fall, it must rise or fall on the basis of Christian orthodoxy as it relates to Nicene Christology. While my vision for this theological reality is predicated upon a Wesleyan view of the freedom of the human will, I do not believe Reformed theology is at all threatened by my arguments. Indeed, if one affirms soteriological determinism (or a softer form like compatibilism) and has a high view of the Holy Spirit's agency, then entire sanctification is surely not outside the realm of doctrinal plausibility within the Reformed sphere of influence—or any other stream of the Christian tradition. Any good Calvinist brother or sister may disagree with various elements of how this doctrine might apply to women and men in ministry as it relates to God's response to patriarchy and the fall, or even how eschatology plays out in the end—but no major Reformed theological distinctive is threatened by this doctrine as far as I can see. Indeed, no orthodox Christian doctrines are endangered by this modest proposal—instead, I would humbly insist that Christian perfection promotes the orthodoxy of classical Christian theology insofar as it relies entirely on an orthodox Trinitarian understanding of Scripture and divine action.

I have said to others that God's perspective of humankind is like being naked in a glass house. God can see everything, God knows everything, and nothing can be hidden from God. As such, a significant aspect of preaching is inviting people to confess their sins. Within a Baptist context, I had the privilege of leading the church through Advent last year and Lent this year, and each time we spent time in silent confession for sin. We are glass houses: confessing our sin is both an act of vulnerability and an act of resignation. There is no place to hide. So, we calm down, collect ourselves as best we can, and profess our sins to God with our brothers and sisters at our side.

On the heels of confession lies the specter of repentance. We confess what we have done, and we ask God's Spirit to cleanse us, to empower us. We have sinned mightily, and we ask God to forgive our sins. We ask that God would purify our hearts so that we can discern his will. We are clay in the hands of the Holy Spirit, and we repent so as to be molded and clothed in Christ's love. When we are clothed, we are reconciled and made new. The old has ceased, the new has taken root. The Holy Spirit will then work with us as we move toward being conformed to Christ. Sin, then, has no chance for survival.

God's ultimate purpose in creation is to be united to us without reservation. The goal of entire sanctification is to strip away the sins that hinder us from full participation in Christ, not to inflate our own egos and desires. As Paul has so eloquently taught us, we are to seek the renewing of our minds and our desires in Christ. What God is doing among us and for us is to put our sins to death and to proclaim us as sons and daughters, fully sanctified and fully beloved by God. As our bodies grow old and we suffer illness and pain, we can be comforted that the Spirit is ever-present, ever-involved in our lives and mental and spiritual health. At the end of all things, sin will not possess any power in our lives and the treasonous act of Christian perfection is God's final victory for us. We have moved from the sovereignty of darkness and into the kingdom of his beloved son (Col 1:13–14); because God has done this, we can now live and participate in the things of God without fear or hesitation—now and forevermore. Imagine a world without sin or death, now. Where God is at work and the fruits of such work are visible in the lives of those who have yielded to the Spirit. Where sin and enslavement are replaced with hope and sanctified joy, where fear and loss and replaced with peace and strength. Where God is present and we will not be afraid of who we are, because at that moment—at that time—we are becoming more like him in every way.

Sanctification is now. Take and live it.

Bibliography

Abraham, William J. "Christian Perfection." In *The Oxford Handbook of Methodist Studies*, edited by James E. Kirby and William J. Abraham, 587–601. Oxford: Oxford University Press, 2011.

Abraham, William J., and David F. Watson. *Key United Methodist Beliefs*. Nashville: Abingdon, 2013.

Baker, Lynn Rudder. "Christian Materialism in a Scientific Age." https://www.google.com/url?sa=t&rct=j&q=&esrc=s&source=web&cd=3&ved=0ahUKEwj97pbt4ojcAhWHGDQIHVN6AHoQFgg2MAI&url=https%3A%2F%2Fpeople.umass.edu%2Flrb%2Ffiles%2Fbak11chris_mat.pdf&usg=AOvVaw3l4zDvdZoVctShy6vXgh8H

Barclay, John M. G. *Paul and the Gift*. Grand Rapids: Eerdmans, 2015.

Bates, Matthew W. *Salvation by Allegiance Alone: Rethinking Faith, Works, and the Gospel of Jesus the King*. Grand Rapids: Baker Academic, 2017.

———. *The Birth of the Trinity: Jesus, God, and Spirit in New Testament & Early Christian Interpretations of the Old Testament*. Oxford: Oxford University Press, 2015.

———. "A Christology of Incarnation and Enthronement: Romans 1:3-4 as Unified, Nonadoptionist, and Nonconciliatory." *Catholic Biblical Quarterly* 77 (2015) 107–27.

Bauckham, Richard. *Gospel Women: Studies of the Named Women in the Gospels*. Grand Rapids: Eerdmans, 2002.

Beker, J. Christiaan. *Paul's Apocalyptic Gospel: The Coming Triumph of God*. Philadelphia: Fortress, 1982.

Belleville, Linda L. *2 Corinthians*. Downers Grove, IL: InterVarsity, 1996.

Berkouwer, G. C. *Studies in Dogmatic: Faith and Sanctification*. Grand Rapids: Eerdmans, 1952.

Bird, Michael F. *Jesus the Eternal Son: Answering Adoptionist Christology*. Grand Rapids: Eerdmans, 2017.

Bird, Michael F., and Preston Sprinkle, eds. *The Faith of Jesus Christ: Exegetical, Biblical, and Theological Studies.* Peabody, MA: Hendrickson, 2009.

Bird Michael F., and Scott Harrower. *Trinity without Hierarchy: Reclaiming Nicene Orthodoxy in Evangelical Theology.* Grand Rapids: Kregel Academic, 2019.

Bultmann, Rudolph. *Theology of the New Testament.* 1 vol. New York: Scribner's Sons, 1951–1955.

Burnett, Daniel L. *In the Shadow of Aldersgate: An Introduction to the Heritage and Faith of the Wesleyan Tradition.* Eugene, OR: Wipf & Stock, 2006.

Bushnell, Katherine C. *God's Word to Women.* Minneapolis: Christians for Biblical Equality, 1923.

Butner, D. Glenn. *The Son Who Learned Obedience: A Theological Case against the Eternal Submission of the Son.* Eugene, OR: Pickwick, 2018.

Calvin, John. *The Second Epistle of the Apostle to the Corinthians and the Epistles to Timothy, Titus and Philemon.* Vol. 10. Translated by T.A. Smail. Grand Rapids: Eerdmans, 1961.

Campbell, Douglas A. *The Deliverance of God: An Apocalyptic Rereading of Justification in Paul.* Grand Rapids: Eerdmans, 2009.

Cervin, Richard S. "A Note Regarding the Name Junia(s) in Romans 16:7." *New Testament Studies* 40 (1994) 464–70.

Cohick, Lynn H. *Women in the World of the Earliest Churches: Illuminating Ancient Ways of Life.* Grand Rapids: Baker Academic, 2009.

Collins, John J. *Apocalypse, Prophecy, and Pseudepigraphy: On Jewish Apocalyptic Literature.* Grand Rapids: Eerdmans, 2015.

Collins, Kenneth J. *The Theology of John Wesley: Holy Love and the Shape of Grace.* Nashville: Abingdon, 2007.

———. *The Scripture Way of Salvation: The Heart of John Wesley's Theology.* Nashville: Abingdon, 1997.

Collins, Raymond C. *Second Corinthians.* Grand Rapids: Baker Academic, 2013.

Cooper, John W. *Body, Soul, and Life Everlasting: Biblical Anthropology and the Monism-Dualism Debate.* Grand Rapids: Eerdmans, 1989.

Corcoran, Kevin J. *Rethinking Human Nature: A Christian Materialism Alternative to the Soul.* Grand Rapids: Baker Academic, 2006.

Crisp, Oliver D. *Saving Calvinism: Expanding the Reformed Tradition.* Downers Grove, IL: InterVarsity Academic, 2016.

———. *Deviant Calvinism: Broadening Reformed Theology.* Minneapolis: Fortress, 2014.

Cutler, Caroline Schleier. "New Creation and Inheritance: Inclusion and Full Participation in Paul's Letters to the Galatians and Romans." *Priscilla Papers* 30 (2016) 21–29.

Davis, John Jefferson. "First Timothy 2:12, the Ordination of Women, and Paul's Use of Creation Narratives." *Priscilla Papers* 23 (2009) 5–10.

Dieter, Melvin E. "The Wesleyan Perspective." In *Five Views on Sanctification*, edited by Stan N. Gundry, 9–46. Grand Rapids: Zondervan, 1987.

Dunn, James D. G. *Christology in the Making: A New Testament Inquiry into the Doctrine of the Incarnation.* Grand Rapids: Eerdmans, 1996.

———. *The Theology of Paul the Apostle.* Grand Rapids: Eerdmans, 1988.

Dunning, H. Ray. "Christian Perfection: Toward a New Paradigm." *Wesley Theological Journal* 33 (1998) 151–63.

Eastman, Susan Grove. *Paul and the Person: Reframing Paul's Anthropology.* Grand Rapids: Eerdmans, 2017.

Erickson, Millard J. *Christian Theology*. Third edition. Grand Rapids: Baker Academic, 2013.
Fee, Gordon D. *The First Epistle to the Corinthians*. Revised edition. Grand Rapids: Eerdmans, 2014.
———. *God's Empowering Presence: The Holy Spirit in the Letters of Paul*. Grand Rapids: Baker Academic, 2009.
———. *Pauline Christology: An Exegetical-Theological Study*. Peabody, MA: Hendrickson, 2007.
———. *Paul's Letter to the Philippians*. Grand Rapids: Eerdmans, 1995.
———. *The First Epistle to the Corinthians*. Grand Rapids: Eerdmans, 1987.
Flemming, Dean. *Philippians: A Commentary in the Wesleyan Tradition*. Kansas City: Beacon Hill, 2009.
Fowl, Stephen. *Philippians*. Grand Rapids: Eerdmans, 2005.
Fudge, Edward William. *The Fire that Consumes: A Biblical and Historical Survey*. Eugene, OR: Wipf & Stock, 2011.
Garland, David E. *1 Corinthians*. Grand Rapids: Baker Academic, 2003.
Goldingay, John. *Biblical Theology: The God of the Christian Scriptures*. Downers Grove, IL: IVP Academic, 2016.
Gorman, Michael J. *Inhabiting the Cruciform God: Kenosis, Justification, and Theosis in Paul's Narrative Soteriology*. Grand Rapids: Eerdmans, 2009.
Greathouse, William M. and George Lyons. *Romans 1–8: A Commentary in the Wesleyan Tradition*. Kansas City: Beacon Hill, 2008.
Green, Joel B. *Body, Soul, and Human Life: The Nature of Humanity in the Bible*. Grand Rapids: Baker Academic, 2008.
Grider, J. Kenneth. *A Wesleyan-Holiness Theology*. Beacon Hill: Kansas City, 1994.
———. *Entire Sanctification: The Distinctive Doctrine of Wesleyanism*. Kansas City: Beacon Hill, 1980.
Grudem, Wayne A. *Systematic Theology: An Introduction to Biblical Doctrine*. Grand Rapids: Zondervan, 1994.
Guthrie, George H. *2 Corinthians*. Grand Rapids: Baker Academic, 2015.
Harris, Murray J. *The Second Epistle to the Corinthians: A Commentary on the Greek Text*. Grand Rapids: Eerdmans, 2005.
———. *Colossians & Philemon*. Grand Rapids: Eerdmans, 1991.
Hays, Richard B. *First Corinthians*. Louisville: Westminster John Knox, 1997.
Hill, Wesley. *Paul and the Trinity: Persons, Relations, and the Pauline Letters*. Grand Rapids: Eerdmans, 2015.
———. *Spiritual Friendship: Finding Love in the Church as a Celibate Gay Christian*. Grand Rapids: Brazos, 2015.
Hitchcock, Christina S. *The Significance of Singleness: A Theological Vision for the Future of the Church*. Grand Rapids: Baker Academic, 2018.
Horton, Michael. *The Christian Faith: A Systematic Theology for Pilgrims on the Way*. Grand Rapids: Zondervan, 2011.
Hübner, Jamin. "Revisiting the Clarity of Scripture in 1 Timothy 2:12." *Journal of the Evangelical Theological Society* 59 (2016) 99–117.
———. "Revisiting αὐθεντέω in 1 Timothy 2:12: What do the Extant Data really show?" *Journal for the Study of Paul and His Letters* 5 (2015) 41–71.
Hurtado, Larry W. *Destroyer of the Gods: Early Christian Distinctiveness in the Roman World*. Waco, TX: Baylor University Press, 2016.

BIBLIOGRAPHY

Jacob, Haley Goranson. *Conformed to the Image of His Son: Reconsidering Paul's Theology of Glory in Romans.* Downers Grove, IL: InterVarsity, 2018.

Jewett, Robert. *Romans.* Minneapolis: Fortress, 2007.

———. *Paul's Anthropological Terms: A Study of Their Use in Conflict Settings.* Leiden: Brill, 1971.

Jipp, Joshua W. "Ancient, Modern, and Future Interpretations of Romans 1:3-4: Reception History and Biblical Interpretation." *Journal of Theological Interpretation* 3 (2009) 241–59.

Johnson, S. Lewis. "Role Distinctions in the Church: Galatians 3:28." In *Recovering Biblical Manhood and Womanhood: A Response to Evangelical Feminism,* edited by John Piper and Wayne Grude, 148-60. Wheaton, IL: Crossway, 1991.

Johnson, W. Stanley. "Christian Perfection as Love for God." *Wesley Theological Journal* 18 (1983) 50–61.

Kärkkäinen, Veli-Matti. *Christ and Reconciliation.* Vol. 1. Grand Rapids: Eerdmans, 2013.

———. *Creation and Humanity.* Vol. 3. Grand Rapids: Eerdmans, 2015.

Longenecker, Bruce W. *Remember the Poor: Paul, Poverty & The Greco-Roman World.* Grand Rapids: Eerdmans, 2010.

Longenecker, Richard N. *The Epistle to the Romans.* Grand Rapids: Eerdmans, 2016.

MacDonald, Gregory. *The Evangelical Universalist.* Second edition. Eugene, OR: Cascade, 2012.

Maddox, Randy L. "John Wesley and Eastern Orthodoxy: Influences, Convergences and Differences." *The Asbury Theological Journal* 45 (1990) 29–53.

Marshall, I. Howard. *Kept by the Power of God: A Study of Perseverance and Falling Away.* Eugene, OR: Wipf & Stock, 2007.

———. *The Pastoral Epistles.* London: T. & T. Clark, 1999.

Martin, Ralph P. *Philippians.* Revised. Waco, TX: Word, 2004.

———. *2 Corinthians.* Vol. 40. Waco, TX: Word, 1986.

McKirland, Matthew and Christa McKirland. "Who's in Charge? Questioning our Common Assumptions about Spiritual Authority." *Priscilla Papers* 27 (2013) 15–25.

McKnight, Scot. *The Epistle to the Colossians.* Grand Rapids: Eerdmans, 2018.

Murphy, Nancey. *Bodies and Souls, Or Spirited Bodies?* Cambridge: Cambridge University Press, 2006.

Murphy-O'Connor, Jerome. *The Theology of the Second Letter to the Corinthians.* Cambridge: Cambridge University Press, 1991.

Oden, Thomas C. *John Wesley's Teachings: Christ and Salvation.* Vol. 2. Grand Rapids: Zondervan, 2012.

Outler, Albert C. *John Wesley's Sermons: An Anthology.* Nashville: Abingdon, 1991.

Outler, Albert C., ed. *John Wesley.* New York: Oxford University Press, 1964.

Payne, Philip B. "A Summary of "Vaticanus Distigme-obelos Symbols Marking Added Text, Including 1 Corinthians 14.34-5." *New Testament Studies* 63 (2017) 604–25.

———. *Man and Woman, One in Christ: An Exegetical and Theological Study of Paul's Letters.* Grand Rapids: Zondervan, 2009.

Peckham, John C. *Theodicy of Love: Cosmic Conflict and the Problem of Evil.* Grand Rapids: Baker Academic, 2018.

———. *The Love of God: A Canonical Model.* Downers Grove, IL: InterVarsity, 2015.

Pierce, Ronald W. "First Corinthians 7: Paul's Neglected Treatise on Gender." *Priscilla Papers* 23 (2009) 8–13.

Porter, Stanley E. *The Letter to the Romans: A Linguistic and Literary Commentary.* Sheffield: Sheffield Phoenix, 2015.

———. *Idioms of the Greek New Testament.* 2nd edition. Sheffield: Sheffield Academic, 1994.

———. "The Argument of Romans 5: Can a Rhetorical Question Make a Difference?" *Journal of Biblical Literature* 110 (1991) 655–77.

Quient, Allison M. "*Eve Christology: Embodiment, Gender and Salvation.*" *Canadian-American Theological Review.* Forthcoming.

Quient, Nicholas Rudolph. "Destruction from the Presence of the Lord: Paul's Intertextual Use of the LXX in 2 Thess. 1:9." A paper presented at the Rethinking Hell Conference in London, UK, 7–8, in October 2016.

———. "Paul's God of Peace: Greetings and the Rhetoric of Gender in Romans 16." *Journal of the Ecclesia Scholars Society.* Accepted for publication 2019.

———. "Was Apphia an Early Christian Leader? An Investigation and Proposal regarding the Woman in Philemon 1:2." *Priscilla Papers* 31 (2017) 10–13.

Seifrid, Mark A. *The Second Letter to the Corinthians.* Grand Rapids: Eerdmans, 2014.

Shelton, W. Brian *Prevenient Grace: God's Provision for Fallen Humanity.* Anderson, IN: Warner, 2014.

Silva, Moisés. *Philippians.* 2nd edition. Grand Rapids: Baker Academic, 2005.

Sproul, R. C. "The Heresy of Perfectionism." *Blog* (Blog) *Ligonier Ministries*, May 10, 2013, http://www.ligonier.org/blog/heresy-perfectionism/.

Stott, John. and Al Hsu. "John Stott on Singleness." *John Stott* (blog), *Christianity Today*, August 17, 2011, https://www.christianitytoday.com/ct/2011/augustweb-only/johnstottsingleness.html.

Stowers, Stanley K. *A Rereading of Romans: Justice, Jews, & Gentiles.* New Haven: Yale University Press, 1994.

Talbott, Thomas. *The Inescapable Love of God.* Second Edition. Eugene, OR: Cascade, 2014.

Thiselton, Anthony C. *The First Epistle to the Corinthians.* Grand Rapids: Eerdmans, 2000.

Thompson, Marianne Meye. *John: A Commentary.* New Testament Library. Louisville: Westminster John Knox, 2015.

———. *Colossians & Philemon.* Grand Rapids: Eerdmans, 2005.

Thornhill, A. Chadwick *The Chosen People: Election, Paul and Second Temple Judaism.* Downers Grove, IL: InterVarsity Academic, 2015.

Thrall, Margaret E. *II Corinthians 8–13: Volume 2. A Critical and Exegetical Commentary.* Edinburgh: T. & T. Clark, 2000.

———. *A Critical and Exegetical Commentary on the Second Epistle to the Corinthians.* Volume 2. Edinburgh: T. & T. Clark, 2000.

Timpe, Kevin. *Free Will in Philosophical Theology.* New York: Bloomsbury, 2014.

Towner, Philip H. *The Letters to Timothy and Titus.* Grand Rapids: Eerdmans, 2006.

Walls, Jerry. *Purgatory: The Logic of Total Transformation.* Oxford: Oxford University Press, 2012.

Wanamaker, Charles A. *The Epistles to the Thessalonians.* Grand Rapids: Eerdmans, 1990.

Wesley, John. *Explanatory Notes upon the New Testament.* New York: Carlton & Porter, n.d.

Westfall, Cynthia Long. *Paul and Gender: Reclaiming the Apostle's Vision for Men and Women in Christ.* Grand Rapids: Baker Academic, 2016.

BIBLIOGRAPHY

Witherington, Ben, III. *1 and 2 Thessalonians: A Socio-Rhetorical Commentary.* Grand Rapids: Eerdmans, 2006.

———. *Conflict and Community in Corinth: A Socio-Rhetorical Commentary on 1-2 Corinthians.* Grand Rapids: Eerdmans, 1995.

Witherington, Ben, III, and Darlene Hyatt. *Paul's Letter to the Romans: A Socio-Rhetorical Commentary.* Grand Rapids: Eerdmans, 2004.

Wright, N. T. *Paul and the Faithfulness of God.* 2 vols. Minneapolis: Fortress, 2013.

———. *Rethinking Heaven, the Resurrection, and the Mission of the Church.* New York: HarperOne, 2008.

Author Index

Abraham, William J., xiv, xivn3, xv, xvi, 2–3, 3n10, 3n11, 6, 6n30, 6n32
Ashworth, J., 58n44

Baker, Lynne Rudder, 33, 33n86
Barclay, John M. G., 57n41
Bates, Matthew W., 15n25, 18, 18n32, 18n34
Bates. Matthew W., 14n23, 17n29
Bauckham, Richard, 82n34
Beker, J. Christiaan, 9, 9n3
Belleville, Linda L., 13n12, 56, 56n39
Berkouwer, G. C., 4n19
Bird, Michael F., 8n1, 16n26, 18, 18n35, 24n62, 45n137
Bultmann, Rudolph, 56n38
Burnett, Daniel L., xiiin2
Bushnell, Katerine, 75–76, 76n15
Butner, D. Glenn, 28n76, 45n137

Calvin, John, 13, 13n16
Campbell, Douglas A., 9, 16n27
Cervin, Richard S., 82n33
Chambers, Talbot B., 58n44
Cohick, Lynn H., 77n20
Collins, John J., 8–9, 8n2

Collins, Kenneth J., xvi, 6, 6n31, 47n1, 102, 102n9
Collins, Raymond C., 13n12
Cooper, John W., 32n84, 38, 38n109, 38n110, 38n113, 39n117, 39n118, 40n119
Corcoran, Kevin J., 33n87
Crisp, Oliver D., 4n20, 43n129
Cutler, Caroline Schleier, 81n31

Davis, John Jefferson, 84n46
Dieter, Melvin E., 3n17
Driscoll, Mark, 73n9
Dunn, James D. G., 10–11, 11n7, 12, 13, 13n17, 29n78
Dunning, H. Ray, xv, xvn5

Eastman, Susan Grove, 36, 36n103
Erickson, Millard J., 105–6, 105n15, 105n16, 105n17

Fee, Gordon D., 14n18, 16n28, 50n11, 52, 61, 61n54, 61n57, 79n27, 80n29, 83n39
Flemming, Dean, 61n55, 62, 62n58, 62n59
Fowl, Stephen, 20n43, 60, 60n49

AUTHOR INDEX

Fudge, Edward William, 90n5

Garland, David E., 23n57
Gaventa, Beverley, 9
Goldingay, John, 31, 31n83
Gorman, Michael J., 15n24, 110, 110n20
Greathouse, William M., 101n6
Green, Joel B., 38-39, 39n114, 40n120
Grider, J. Kenneth, 2n2, 5, 5n26
Grudem, Wayne A., xv, xvn7, 102-5, 102n10, 103n11, 104n12, 106
Guthrie, George H., 13n12

Harris, Murray J., 13n12, 63n60
Harrower, Scott, 24n62, 45n137
Hays, Richard B., 53n29, 73n10, 92n10
Hill, Wesley, 21n51, 21n54, 23n58, 23n61, 71n3
Hitchcock, Christina S., 71n6
Horton, C. F., xvn8
Hsu, Al, 71n5
Hübner, Jamin, 84, 84n42, 84n43
Hunter, Braxton, 45n138
Hurtado, Larry W., 77n21
Hyatt, Darlene, 102n8

Jacob, Haley Goranson, 44n134
Jewett, Robert, 17n30, 20n46, 21n49, 26n70, 35n97, 42n125, 44n134, 49n7, 50, 50n12, 82n38, 95n24
Jipp, Joshua W., 18n33
Johnson, W. Stanley, xiv-xv, xvn4, 80n30

Kärkkäinen, Veli-Matti, 28n74, 28n75, 33, 33n88, 36n100

Lindsey, Hal, 9
Long, Austin, 22n55, 58n44
Longenecker, Bruce W., 1on6
Longenecker, Richard N., 20n46, 51n17
Lyons, George, 101n6

MacDonald, Gregory, 90n4
Maddox, Randy L., 109, 109n19
Marshall, I. Howard, 95n26, 106-7, 107n18

Martin, Ralph P., 12n10, 13n12, 58, 58n45, 59, 61n56
Martyn, J. Louis, 9
McKirland, Matthew and Christa, 79n28
McKnight, Scot, 64, 64n65, 64n66
Murphy, Nancey, 33n85
Murphy-O'Connor, Jerome, 11, 11n8, 11n9, 12

Oden, Thomas C., 5, 5n25
Outler, Albert C., 67n75

Payne, Philip B., 83n41, 84, 84n43, 84n44, 84n46
Peckham, John C., 44n132
Pierce, Ronald W., 72n8
Porter, Stanley E., 17n31, 20, 20n46, 42n125, 50n10
Pritchett, Johnathan, 45n138

Quient, Allison, 84, 84n45
Quient, Nicholas Rudolph, 82n36, 82n37, 93n15

Schaff, Philip, 58n44
Seifrid, Mark A., 13n12
Shelton, W. Brian, 65n71
Silva, Moisés, 60, 60n51, 60n52
Sprinkle, Preston, 16n26
Sproul, R. C., xv, xvn6, 100-102, 100n2, 100n3-101n3, 101n4, 104, 106
Stott, John, 71n5
Stowers, Stanley K., 101n7

Talbott, Thomas, 90n4
Thiselton, Anthony C., 52, 52n22, 53n24, 53n28, 63n62, 92, 92n11
Thompson, Marianne Meye, 4n18, 64, 64n64
Thornhill, A. Chadwick, 41n122, 44n134, 51n16
Thrall, Margaret E., 13, 13n13, 13n14
Timpe, Kevin, 44n136
Towner, Philip H., 96n27

Walls, Jerry L., 44n136, 90n3
Wanamaker, Charles A., 36n101, 66n74

AUTHOR INDEX

Watson, David F., 6, 6n32
Wesley, John, xvi, 1–3, 5, 12, 13n17, 34n93, 38n111, 42n126, 43n128, 47, 49n4, 54, 54n30, 57, 57n42, 59, 59n46, 65n70, 66n72, 67
Westfall, Cynthia Long, 23n59, 24n63, 63n62, 70n1, 74, 74n13, 77n23, 78n25, 84, 84n43, 84n46, 85, 85n48, 85n49
Witherington, Ben, III, 36n101, 54n35, 56, 56n37, 56n38, 81n32, 102n8
Wright, N. T., 9n5, 13, 13n15

Scripture Index

Old Testament

Genesis

1:1	26, 26n69
1-3	85
1:26-28	30
3:12	84
28:4	25n66
31:14	25n66

Exodus

6:6	26n68
19:23	66
29:1, 33, 36	66
29:1-35	49n6

Leviticus

6:21	31n80
11:33	31n80
14:50	31n80
15:12	31n80

Numbers

20:12	66
27:11	25n66
27:14	66

1 Kings

19:10	34
19:10-14	34n91

2 Kings

8:61	62
11:4	62
15:3	62
20:3	62

2 Chronicles

2:3	66

SCRIPTURE INDEX

Psalms

8:7	23n61
17:48	21
33:7	11
51:11	27
109:1	91
109:5-6	91n7
110	23n61
146:4	35

Ecclesiastes

12:7	2

Song of Songs

	74

Isaiah

2:10-21	93
11:4	92n13

Jeremiah

3:19	25n66
48:8	94n18
51:55	94n18

Ezekiel

18:31	35

Daniel

	8

Habakkuk

2:4	16

Deuterocanonical Books

Tobit

1:17	40
3:6	38

Judith

6:4	94
9:7	91
16:2	91

1 Maccabees

1:30	94
3:42	94
4:32	91
11:18	94
12:1	44

2 Maccabees

	19n40
8:7	44
8:9, 22	21
12:7	19n40
12:28	91
12:42	49
14:5	44

Wisdom

1:11	34
12:1	95
12:6	84
18:4	95
18:5	94

Sirach

6:4	34

13:2	91n8
21:2	34
27:2	91n8
34:8	49
34:18	51n15
35:5	51n15
46:16	51n15
50:13	51n15

1 Esdras

1:3	66
7:2	44n133

4 Ezra 8

4 Maccabees

18:11	92

Odes

1:3	91
7:38	51n15
7:44	91

Psalms of Solomon

16:13-14	37

Pseudepigrapha

2 Baruch 8

Testament of Judah

25.4	12

New Testament

Matthew

3:6	67
3:11	67
4:1	27n73
5:43	3
5:48	64
7:13	94n20
10:28	34n92, 36n102, 94n20
19:1ff	75
19:3	75
28:19	27
28:19-20	81

Mark

1:12	27n73
3:4	34
9:24	17
10:1-12	75
10:40	20n42

Luke

1:15	27
1:35	27
4:1	27n73
7:25	76n17
8:1-3	71
8:3	82n34
13:17	76n17
24:10	82n34

John

1:9	30
4:34	4
5:36	4
17:4	4
17:23	4
21:18-19	61

SCRIPTURE INDEX

Acts

2:28	81
2:36	17
2:38	27
13:33	17

Romans — 9, 9n4, 82

1:1	82, 82n35
1:1-4	17
1:3-4	17, 18, 20n45
1:16	41
1:17	16
1:23	95
2:6-7	56
2:7	33, 96
2:9	33
2:9	33n90
2:12	33
2:27	48n3
3:21-26	62
3:22	15, 16, 41
3:25	6
4:4-5	41
5:1	42
5:5	27, 51
5:12	29, 84
5:12-21	13n17, 18, 101
5:12-21ff	42
5:17	43
5:17, 21	18
5:19	15
6	4
6:3-4	67, 81
6:4	43
6:6	29, 48, 93
6:8	41
6:11	4
6:19-22	49
6:23	91
7	29, 29n77, 100, 101, 102, 105
7:7-13	29, 101
7:7-25	13n17, 29, 39n116
7:7b	102
7:8	102
7:9	101n5
7:10	101n5
7:10-11	102
7:13	29
7:24	102
8	105
8:1	39n116, 102
8:1-11	18n37
8:7	30
8:9-11	21
8:9b	21
8:9c	21
8:11	21
8:15	27
8:18-23	88
8:20	20, 22n55, 30
8:20-21	89
8:23	30n79, 47
8:27	51
8:28	44, 44n134
8:29	60
9	41n122
9:1	51
9:5	21n49
9-11	51
9:30-32	41
10:3	30
11:2	33
11:3	33
11:13	82
11:32-36	51
12:1-2	49, 50, 111
12:2	68
12:4-5	36
13:1	34
13:7	48
13:12	40
13:14	40
14:17	27, 51
15:6	50
15:6a	50
15:13	51
15:16	27, 49, 51, 68
16	71, 82, 82n38
16:2	82
16:3, 9, 21	44

16:4	34, 82	7:14-16	74
16:4b	34n94	7:34	53
16:7	82	8:6	25n67
16:20	90–91, 91	9:19-22	37n106
		10:13	5
		11:2-16	84n47

1 Corinthians 9, 9n4, 54, 55, 83

1:2	52	11:5	84n47
1:8	52	11:10	84n47
1:10-11	52	12:4	79
1:18	94	12:4-6	79
1:28	92n10, 93n14	12:7b	79
1:30	47, 52	12:11	79
2:6	49, 53, 92, 93n14	12:12	79
2:16	53	12:12-27	36
3:9	44	12:13	67
3:9b	44n135	12-14	79, 80
3:15-17	53n25	12:23	80
3:17	53	13:5	43
3:17b	44n135	13:10	54n34
4:10	76n17	14:20	54n34
5:1	72	14:33	52n21
5:6	40	14:34-35	83
5:6-9	40	14:40	83
5:7	41	15	13n17
5:10	41	15:1-8	82n34
6:1-2, 19	53	15:20-28	20, 21n51, 22, 43n127
6:1-20	53	15:24	53, 92
6:5	53	15:24-26	49, 68, 91–93
6-7	53, 54	15:24-28	23
6:9-10	54	15:25-28	20
6:11	27n72, 54	15:26	36, 92
6:12	29	15:28	23
6:15	36	15:35	18n37
7	53, 78	15:35-57	39, 59n47
7:1	72	15:42-55	35, 96n28
7:1-16	54, 72, 75, 76	15:53-54	40
7:2	72	16:1, 15, 20	52n21
7:3	72		
7:3-5	77, 84		

2 Corinthians 54, 58

1:1	52n21, 55n36
1:12	55
1:23	34n96
1:24	44
2:15	94
4:3	31

7:4	72
7:5	72
7:6-9	73
7:7-9	71
7:10-11	73
7:14	54

2 Corinthians (*continued*)

4:3ff	31
4:4	29, 47
4:7	31
4:8-10	31
4:10	31
4:11	31
4:16	31, 47
4:18	31
5:1-5	39n117
5:1-10	30–31, 36, 38n109, 39
5:3	40
5:4	40
5:5-6	40n121
5:16-17	81
5:17	59, 85, 89
6:1	44
6:4-6	55
6:6	55
6:14_7:1	56n38
6:14-18	57
7:1	56, 57, 58, 59, 64, 68, 77n24, 89, 102, 103
8	10
8:1-11	10
8:2	10
8:4	52n21, 55n36
8:6b	10
8:9	10, 11, 13, 14, 15, 17, 45
8:23	44
9:1, 12	52n21, 55n36
12:9	55
12:15	34n96
13:12	52n21
13:13	55n36
13:21	55n36

Galatians

1-2	1
1:4	41
2:16	16, 41, 42
2:16a	16, 42
2:16b	42
2:16c	42
2:17a	42, 43
2:20	43
3:3	56n40
3:22	15, 16, 41
3:26-29	80, 81, 98
3:27	40, 67
3:28	29, 80
3:28-29	81
4:3	18
4:4	14n21, 18
5:16-17	43
5:18-23	55
6:8	94n19
6:15	89

Ephesians

1:19	43
1:20-23	24
1:22	29, 63n61
2:2	29
2:11-22	23
2:25	23
2:27	23, 23n59
4:5	67, 81
4:7	47
4:14-16	24n63
4:23	47
5:1-2	77
5:5	24, 25, 96n27
5:5-6	22
5:21	76
5:21-24	23n60
5:21-33	24n63, 71, 75, 78
5:22	75, 76, 76n18
5:22f	76
5:23-24	76, 76n19
5:25	70
5:25-30	76
5:27b	22n56
5:28	78, 78n25
5:29	78
5:31	25n65
6:2	25n65
6:4	25n65

6:6	34n96	Colossians	9n4
6:11-14	40		
6:12	29	1:9	65
6:24	97	1:10	63
		1:13-14	113
		1:13-20	24, 25–26
Philippians	xiv	1:13b	26
		1:14	64
1	37, 38	1:14-20	65n69
1:5	60	1:15	6, 26, 64
1:6	39, 57, 60	1:15-20	26n69, 47, 62, 89
1:7,13-14, 17	37	1:16	25n64, 26, 63
1:12-13	43	1:18	63
1:13	37	1:19	65
1:17	37	1:19-20	64
1:19	37	1:20-22	62
1:20-24	36, 37, 38n109, 38n112, 39n115	1:21	62
		1:23	62
1:23	38	1:27	63
1:27	34n96	1:28	62, 63, 64, 65, 68
2	37, 43	1:29	63
2:3	37	2:9	16, 65, 65n69
2:4	18	2:10	63, 65
2:4-5	62	2:10, 19	63
2:5-11	13–14, 13n17, 15, 17	2:12	67, 81
2:5a	43–44	2:14	64
2:6-7	14, 43	2:19	63
2:6-8	14, 17n31, 24, 61n54	3:1-4	19, 39
2:8	15, 19	3:10-12	40
2:25	44	3:11	29
2:25-30	37n106	3:12-13	64
2:30	34n96	3:14	62, 63
3:3-4	38	3:23	34n96
3:9	61	4:11	44
3:10	61, 61n54	4:12	62, 64–65, 68
3:11	39, 61, 62		
3:11b	39n115		
3:12	1, 61, 62	1 Thessalonians	35
3:12-15	58, 59, 60, 61, 68, 104		
3:15	62	1:5-6	35
3:19	94	2:8	34n96, 35
3:20	38	2:10	66
3:20-21	19, 20, 37, 38	3:2	44
3:21	19, 21, 38n112, 61	3:13	65n68
4:2-3	82	4:3-5	74n12
4:3	44	4:8	35
		4:13-18	36n104

1 Thessalonians (*continued*)

4:13ff	36n104
5:8	40
5:19	35
5:22	66
5:23	34–35, 66, 102n10, 103
5:24	106

2 Thessalonians

1:9	93
2:7-10	92
2:8	92
2:10	93

1 Timothy

1:16	96
1:17	95
2:4-6	17, 42
2:11	84
2:12	83, 84
2:13-15	84
2:22	59
3:16	15
6:16	96

2 Timothy

1:10	36, 96
2:2	79
2:8	18n36
2:18-22	58
2:21	43, 58

Titus

2:7	97

Philemon

1, 24	44
2	82
vv. 12-14	41

Hebrews

1:3	57
2:10	4
2:14-15	91, 98
5:8	42n124
6:4-6	106
7:19	4
10:14	4

James

3:2	104n12

2 Peter

1:4	59

1 John

1:8	102n10, 103n10
2:1-2	103n10
2:2	103n10
2:5	4
3:6, 9	102n10
4:12, 17, 18	4

xiv 84n43

Early Christian Writings

Ambrosiaster

Commentary on Paul's Epistles

CSEL 81.247   57–58, 58n43

Basil the Great

Concerning Baptism

FC 9:374   60, 60n48

Exegetical Homilies   11

Chrysostom, John

"Homilies of St. John Chrysostom, Archbishop of Constantinople on the Second Epistle of St. Paul the Apostle to the Corinthians"   58n44

Greco-Roman Writings

Pliny the Elder

Natural History

35–36   14

Jewish Writings

Philo

De opficio mundi

1:82   95, 95n25
1:119   95, 95n25

Quod deterius potiori insidiari

1.78   84

www.ingramcontent.com/pod-product-compliance
Lightning Source LLC
Chambersburg PA
CBHW071510150426
43191CB00009B/1470